They Call Me Fero

Reflections and Recollections
of an Iranian-American Doctor

ISBN: 1453600043
ISBN-13: 9781453600047

They Call Me Fero

Reflections and Recollections of an Iranian-American Doctor

F Fero Sadeghian

For Nancy, Scott, Tracy, Mark, and Todd

*"Life is not measured by the number of days lived,
but by the number of days remembered."*

— Iranian proverb

CONTENTS

Pt. IV — Nancy

Pt. V — Retirement and Reflection

Pt. VI — View from the Mountain Top

ACKNOWLEDGEMENTS

Without my wife's generous support in providing the time, and my daughter's unconditional reinforcement, writing of this memoir would not have been possible.

I like to thank my editor Malcolm Mathews for his insightful suggestions, and my high school friend Dr. Zia Ahari for his helpful feedback.

I am indebted to David and Nancy Nyberg for their uncompromising support.

My thanks to Jorge Guitart and Bruce Jackson for their feedback and encouraging words.

I am also grateful for the support of my colleagues and friends, Dr. Laura Ureta, Dr. Mary McGorray, and Lindsay Arthur.

My sincere thanks to Tricia Semmelhack, Julie Baumgold, and Edward Kosner for their guidance.

— F. Fero Sadeghian
East Aurora N.Y

Pt. I – Life Begins in Iran

I. VOICES OF THE LIVING

W hen I meet someone for the first time, I am almost always asked about my name. Invariably, I have to spell it out to avoid confusion with the more well-known "Pharaohs" of Egypt.

At birth, I was named after the mythic hero Fraydoon who captured a terrible monster that supposedly embodied the darkness and evil of the world. Fraydoon chained this monster in a rocky cave at the summit of Mt. Damavand, a dormant volcano and Persia's version of Mt. Olympus. According to the Persian poem "Shahnameh," Fraydoon's heroism gave goodness and benevolence an upper hand in the battle between the opposing forces of darkness and light, a prevalent theme within Zoroastrianism.

During the time I grew up and lived in Iran, very few Zoroastrians lived there anymore. Islam had become the official religion of the country, and most of my peers had Arabic names or names that had a significant religious connotation. "Fraydoon" fell into neither of these categories, and I certainly didn't feel especially epic, religious, or heroic.

Because my name was a mouthful, I quickly became known by its abbreviated form of "Ferri." Later, when I lived in England where my full name remained a tongue-twister and the nickname "Ferri" conjured unpleasant images of a homosexual dandy, people settled for "Fero." When I discovered that "fero" in Latin means "to carry or move forward," I accepted the new name and, brimming with optimism, hoped I could live up to it.

As I grew older, I navigated my way through an exhausting but stimulating adulthood that took me from the peaks of the Himalayas to the expansive glaciers of New Zealand to the inner recesses of the human heart. Along the way, I decided that living up to one's name was too hard, so I decided to turn my attention to living life to the fullest and letting my name live up to me.

In an act of political symbiosis, my birth country of Persia underwent a seemingly radical name change of its own, although the "new" name was as ancient as the country's 5,000 year history, and in 1935 became "Iran." The country's new name was supposed to highlight the historical origin of the Aryan tribes which had inhabited the Iranian steppe at the dawn of our civilization and to portray the country as the land of Aryans. Instead, the new name created misconceptions among the world's nations, which often confused it with the similar sounding but ethnically different Arab nation of Iraq. In 1930, Nazi propaganda contributed to the confusion by falsely claiming the Aryans as a superior race with certain specific and exclusive characteristics of physiognomy as opposed to the true distinctive traits of their language, which spread from the Iranian steppe to the Indus Valley and beyond to Europe and became one of the principal foundations of the Indo-European languages. Fears that the name change might further separate the people from their past, Mohamed Reza Shah announced in 1959 that the names of "Iran" and "Persia" were both acceptable and could be used interchangeably.

In my mind, I have always gone back to Persia, a land of duality, contradiction, and compromise. A land out of the middle ages but replete with serenity, simplicity, and tolerance. Even today in my daily interactions, I see in the faces of complete strangers the same faces I saw in the dusty alleys of southern Tehran during my childhood. This mysterious but welcome human connectedness has made the world a familiar and comforting place, allowing me to move around with ease, helping me to feel at home in my travels, wherever in the world they might take me.

Such familiarity, however, has not necessarily provided a complete sense of belonging and assimilation. As much as I have felt at home in this world, I have remained an outsider at the same time. I have looked up at the starry heavens throughout this journey and have been fortunate to avoid the gaping crevasses.

My quest for spiritual harmony has been a long and rewarding one, dating back, as so many things do, to Persia. Although many elements of my life as a child were appealing, I felt greatly bothered by the depth of corruption of the ruling class and by the extreme resignation of the masses, content with their narrow lot in life. And then, as much as I have admired and loved my adopted country of the United States, after a while I began to see the inevitable social cracks and political blemishes there as well.

Nevertheless, the United States has become my home even though it continues to share my heart with a complex and at times conflict-filled nation on the other side of the world. The urge to reconcile a split heart and two homes came about after listening to a tape recording of my graduating class from medical school.

In 1988 I was in Los Angeles for a surgical conference. While there, I visited my medical school friend Saeed who had left Iran and his successful practice of obstetric gynecology after the Revolution. He had recently started a family practice in California.

After the conference, Saeed and I went for a drive past the manicured California suburbs and their ubiquitous flowering bushes. We drove through the palm-flanked streets and past the lines of citrus trees, which gradually gave way to smaller and smaller versions of themselves as we drove deeper into the desert. The ocher hills morphed in the distance into snow-covered mountain peaks, reminiscent of Iran where I had lived for the first twenty-five years of my life.

With the windows down, Saeed held up a small plastic cartridge and asked above the wind, "Would you like to listen to a tape of our classmates from medical school?"

I asked him, "What tape?"

"A taping of our graduation speeches. Dr. Rokney, one of our old classmates, sent it to me. Do you remember him?"

I thought hard but couldn't picture the man Saeed was talking about.

"He recorded it in the interns' quarter of Pahlavi hospital during the last days of our internship." Saeed pushed the cassette into the tape deck.

For a decades old tape, it was surprisingly clear without any static. Curious, I listened intently.

In their farewell remarks some classmates lamented the imminent departure from the school that had become their second home. They insisted those six years were possibly the happiest times of their lives. Others predicted brighter and happier days ahead. The dominant theme expressed by this diverse group of new graduates was a common concern for humanity and the desire to soothe human misery.

Within a few transforming moments, memories from forty years ago rushed to the surface of my mind, and I found myself oddly mesmerized, captivated by the now-familiar voices of the distant past. My own voice came back to me over the tape. I heard myself and my classmates speak about our concerns, our hopes, and our limitless futures. In my mind's eye, I saw the face of each speaker who until moments earlier had been lost in the past.

As Saeed and I drove along, we listened in silence to the recorded voices. People often talk about ghosts and about hearing the voices of the dead. In the car, listening to Saeed's tape, I did hear ghosts from the past, but they were also the voices of the living. With their positive energy and unqualified hope for the future, there was nothing dead about them.

In my mind, I was back in the bustling, vibrant atmosphere of the interns' living quarters with the oppressive summer heat permeating the narrow corridors. A wobbly ceiling fan clunked in a slow, helpless circle. Interns came and went through swinging doors. The metallic ping of ringing phones echoed along with the voice of the orderly calling the names of interns from hall to hall. Persian music from one room and classical music from another mingled with the music of Nat King Cole and rolled in lyrical waves through the hospital corridors. The smell of saffron, fenugreek, and cumin from the dining hall mixed with the sterilized hospital odor. I thought about my own past. As a boy, I loved adventures and had longed to see the world. I registered in the Naval Academy with the understanding that I would be going to England for training as a sailor. But as fate would have it, I became a doctor.

2. ROOFTOP REFLECTIONS

The Persia of my childhood was a sleepy and isolated country where time hadn't moved for centuries and where hardships of daily life resembled the Middle Ages. Yet, despite their meager lot, Persians accepted their lives with serenity, and they endured hardships with exceptional tolerance.

As a child, I spent a lot of time watching clouds and conjuring my own fantastic worlds. From the comfort of my mattress on the rooftop where I slept in the summer, I watched the rising sun spread its fingers across the horizon with shades of red, pink, orange, and yellow before fading into the silvery white of early morning. I followed the flight of domestic pigeons in the sky, fascinated by how they soared, envious of their freedom. In my mind's eye I flew with them, wondering what lay beyond the limits of my vision. I imagined fantastic scenes of far off places The possibility and promise of seeing those places someday warmed my heart.

On the rooftop of my grandmother's house where I spent good deal of time, when the sky was softer blue, the moon less radiant, and the twinkling of the stars less perceptible, I heard the sound of the passing caravans carrying produce to the market. In the stillness of those early hours, I listened to the tinkling bells of the caravan as it came closer before it faded away with the same slow, undulating rhythm as it made its way to the far side of the city.

I knew that the familiar clump of my grandmother's wooden clogs would not be far behind as she crossed the yard toward the small pool to perform her ablution, the ritual washing of the face, hands, and feet in preparation for her morning prayers.

My grandmother was a small, pear-shaped woman, religious with wavy black hair that she braided at the back in a long mouse tail. Her world revolved around Islam. I don't think she ever laughed. Her fanatical and uncompromising devotion to Islam made a "normal" life quite difficult. For her, many things were *Nages*, or unclean. These unclean objects required repeated washing. Pretty much everything in my parents' household, including me, was considered *najes*. My grandmother did not touch suspicious items with her bare hands. Instead, she used the corner of her dress as a kind of improvised glove. She did not come to our home and did not eat our food. She led a stoic and ascetic life. More often than not, her meals consisted of bread and boiled potatoes. Occasionally she ate rice that had been boiled in milk and mixed with syrup, which she purchased from a shop a few doors away.

Her husband, my grandfather, was a tall imposing figure with a white beard and thinning hair. They called him Arbaab, a feudalistic title identifying him as a property owner. But his personal wealth was unstable. He borrowed from Peter to pay Paul, always hustling to meet his growing daily expenses. His marriage to my grandmother resulted in four children. Then he married a second wife, fathering another four children, and then a third wife gave him two more children. Eventually my grandfather lived with his fourth wife, a younger woman with bleached-blond hair who played the tar, a stringed instrument like a guitar, and shared his love for vodka. He was not a religious man and never prayed unless for show, yet he remained active in most religious ceremonies and always mingled among the community leaders in the front row. A non-believer and consummate hypocrite, he still could not free himself from the tentacles of religion.

For many of my peers, this prevalent Iranian trait remained a primary source of considerable disappointment. The Islam of practice seldom reconciled with the Islam of theory. This chasm led to a delicate social balancing act. Afraid to step too far one way or the other, many throughout the country relinquished a certain love for life. For a nation with thousands of years of political and ideological turbulence and repeated foreign invasions, we felt this adaptability, an ability to sway back and forth within the confines of religion, had gone beyond tolerance and open-mindedness; it bordered now on spinelessness and apathy.

Perhaps reflective of the turmoil and contradictions that characterized the nation as a whole, life in my family was beset by internal tension.

I escaped from the tumultuous relationship of my parents as often as I could and went to my grandmother, herself deserted by her husband, and now living a lonely and frugal life. I knew well that awaiting me there was the same dark room with the same lukewarm welcome and very little food. But the emotionally cold and monastic poverty of my grandmother's home was the only refuge I knew.

Although there was very little about my grandmother's place to look forward to, my imagination, vivid and full of hope as it was, made the thirty-minute walk to her house a pleasant diversion.

I knew the shops and the shopkeepers along the way: The stall for fresh vegetables and fruit. My uncle's pharmacy, which was always crowded with sick people. The man who sold ice cream in the summers and baked sweet turnips in winters. The leprous-looking popcorn sellers. And Mr. Shoa the barber, forever sharpening his old razor blade, the type that slid out of the white handle, against a leather strop.

But my favorite was the pastry shop next to my grandmother's house. Regardless of how many times I passed it, I always stopped to gaze at the display of crème cones behind the window and dream of a taste of the sweetness lying just beyond the glass.

My grandmother lived in a big house next to the tantalizing pastry shop and beyond the market. She lived in one side of the house and her brother, with a large family of six children around my age, lived in the other side.

One day, during a game of hide and seek, I decided to hide in one of the clay containers my grandmother kept in her basement for storing dry grain. I slipped down through its narrow neck and, squatting half down, placed the round metallic cover over the opening from inside. I got the idea of hiding in a large container from the illustrations of *Ali Baba and the Forty Thieves*. Squeezed into my dark space, I waited patiently. Not much later, against the background of the giggles and laughter of my cousins, I heard the heavy footsteps and the angry voice of my uncle approaching the clay container and bellowing my name. The round cover dangling on my head, I stood up, and a wicked slap to my face dislodged me from the jar's narrow opening. I flew clear out of the large urn and across the room, landing heavily on my backside.

In my grandmother's house, if you didn't know where to draw the line yourself, someone older and stronger was sure to draw it for you.

Despite some pretty strict rules, her home drew me not only because of the playmates living in the other side, but also for the spiritual serenity that comforted me and lured me away from the tumultuous life of my parents.

Although she was materially poor, my grandmother remained a tower of spiritual strength. She was independent and indifferent about worldly affairs. Her serenity and internal peace, her spiritual strength, and her pious, ascetic life were contagious. They deeply affected me, and I tried hard to emulate them. I spent much of my childhood between the ages of seven and eleven at her house. I listened to her loud praying and her reading from the Koran so often that such moments have become permanent fixtures in my memory.

I am awake in the cold, early morning hours. I hear the faint click-clack of her wooden clogs as she walks toward the pool at the middle of the yard. She is on her way to wash her hands, face, and feet for her morning prayers. She breaks the thin layer of ice that covers the pool. I know her routine as sure as if it were my own. She washes her face and her hands up to the elbows first, then the crown of her head and finally her feet. Returning, she opens the squeaky door. A rush of cold air sweeps in along with a sliver of the starless sky. She puts on her white prayer gown. It covers everything but the middle circle of her face. She stands in front of the praying mat, facing Mecca. At the center of the mat, there is a rectangular piece of ocher clay, a symbolic representation of Kaaba, the holiest shrine for Moslems. She begins her prayers. Though I do not quite understand the meanings, I know some parts of her prayers by heart as well as the inflections and undulations of her recital. Her face looks different now, no longer tight. Her eyebrows and forehead are unknotted. She kneels, touching her forehead against the stone, sitting up again, absorbed in her world: simple, serene, content. I close my eyes and fall asleep, listening to her conversation with God..

This was the only time in my life when I also prayed and felt the uplifting benefits of internal supplication and a genuine sense of well-being.

Islam's spiritual nurturing and ability to mitigate the injustices of life must have imbued my grandmother. Tolerant and pious, she led a simple, content, and serene life. She possessed what Balzac described as *"La misere a pour elle une devine sommeille plein de beaux rêves."* That sleep full of the marvelous dreams of poverty.

I find it hard to understand or to accept the demonization of the Muslim community as we see so often in the media today. Muslims are tolerant, approachable, and quite capable of living in peace with western nations. The collision course of Islam with the western world, so loudly touted by some, is a polarizing voice of fanaticism that one unfortunately sees in all religions and nations.

Islam is not a homogeneous entity. There are variations and nuances within the religion, some vastly different from the others.

To paint the world of Islam with the same broad brush, seems inappropriate and uncalled-for.

Unlike the unhappy life of my parents and the monastic, lonely life of my grandmother, my great-grandparents lived on an island of serenity. Both of my great-grandparents were in their nineties, totally devoted, respectful, and full of consideration for each other.

I see my great-grandfather coming home in a sunset from his brick factory, cane in hand but still moving at a good pace. His black cap is pushed back, revealing the paler scalp beyond his bronze, sun-beaten face, his deep-set eyes squinting behind small round glasses. He washes and changes into a loose cotton shirt and pants. Sitting cross-legged in front of the white tablecloth where my great-grandmother has carefully arranged his dinner, he leans on his left hand for support and begins his evening meal. Everything is still. All I hear is the heartbeat of the clock on the wall above me. I must be five or six years old. I am fascinated by the butterflies and flowers carved into the tall crystal that covers the oil lamp.

My religious upbringing involved a hodge-podge of dogma ranging from my father's atheism to my grandmother's piety to my grandfather's hypocritical religious lip-service.

During my mother's childhood in the early 1900s, the tight grip of Islam dominated the country and significantly limited the role of women in society. Women were scarcely allowed to leave the house. Higher education beyond primary school was available to very few. My mother was among the first women in the country to graduate from high school. She taught school for a while herself before marrying my father.

My mother's outrage about the lack of opportunity for women in that oppressive religiously dominated culture remained strong throughout her life. She did not practice or show any real religious tendencies until later, after her separation from my father, when she embraced religion as a respite to soothe the bitter experiences of her married life.

And even then, devoted as she was to Islam in her later life, I heard her frequent diatribes against the ignorance and misinterpretation of the Koran by the ruling clergies. Unlike most who read the Koran without any knowledge of the Arabic in which it was originally written, and reliant on interpretation by mullahs, my mother actually understood the language. She felt the brand of Islam practiced and advocated by some of the fanatical ruling mullahs in Iran to be a distortion of her understanding of the religion's central principles.

Religion played no role in my father's side of the family. I never saw any of them go to mosque or pray. They accepted Islam as a fact of life, never critical but silently disapproving. They were blue-eyed, fair-skinned, and of uncertain ethnic origin. I heard my paternal great-grandfather had come from the North, perhaps from Russia or Europe. He converted to Sufism, the most secular version of Islam. My grandfather's premature death at the age of forty from typhoid fever left my father, then just a teenager himself, as the sole provider for his mother, sister, and a younger brother.

At the time of his death, my grandfather co-owned a trading company. But since there was no one to claim it on his behalf, the ownership was taken over by a crooked partner who ended up leaving my grandfather's family in dire financial straits. My grandfather owned substantial parcels of land, which were eventually confiscated by the government of Reza Shah. Years later, I saw wads of deeds for lands and properties near and around Tehran titled under his name. But by then there was no legal recourse since the usurper had been a dictator and was therefore, of course, completely above the law.

In spite of financial hardship, my father and his younger brother continued their education in the Institute de Franco-Persian.

By misrepresenting his age in order to be eligible for employment, my father found a job after graduation in the Ministry of Telephone & Telegraph and became the sole provider for his mother and siblings. His brother was accepted into the French Naval Academy and, after graduation, left the country for France.

The elite graduates of the Institute de Franco, Persians who represented the crème de la crème of a nation with a notoriously low literacy rate, formed the backbone of the intellectuals and played a central role in shaping the future of the country.

Newly employed, my father moved his mother and sister into a small home, a notch higher in status than the previous appalling neighborhood. My mother moved in as the new bride and, for the first time, met Manuchehr, my father's five-year-old son from a previous marriage.

Working night shifts, my father attended law school during the day. After graduation, he was transferred to the Ministry of Justice. He spent over thirty years in the Ministry, most of it as a member of the highest court in the country. He had an impeccable reputation for honesty and integrity, appropriate, considering his name, which means "One Who Speaks the Truth." Following retirement from the Ministry of Justice he practiced law and served as a translator of official French and English documents.

During his tenure in the Ministry of Justice, he continued his education and obtained his Doctorate in Jurisprudence. He spoke French and Persian fluently and had excellent command of both English and Arabic. He had an insatiable thirst for knowledge and remained dedicated to learning throughout his life. He was a worldwide armchair traveler who never left Iran.

At home, my father sat on the floor leaning against a cushion, always with a book in hand. At one point he even got interested in Persian calligraphy. He sang often, usually after his nap and the afternoon tea. He had a good voice and knew the traditional Persian songs. He never saw a doctor and did not believe in taking medicine. For his frequent headaches, he wrapped a scarf around his head. Reluctant to engage in physical activity, he remained sedentary throughout his life. He loved Persian carpets and exotic, European cuisine. Our home was full of colorful carpets, some hanging on the walls, others stacked in piles on the floor. We never knew what to expect from my father's shopping sprees. He would come home with huge quantities of food, much more than we needed but always purchased at bargain prices. Once he brought home an enormous load of watermelon, which he brought in on the back of a donkey. Another time he came home accompanied by porters carrying crates of oranges and enough cheese to feed an army.

My father was approachable and open to discuss any subject. He offered me my first glass of wine and my first cigarette. I don't remember him ever asking me for a favor. Years later, after he bought me a car, if I happened to see him waiting for a taxi and stopped to give him a ride, the first thing he would ask was if I needed my tank filled.

Once a year, the high government officials, senior army officers, and high-court judges went to pay homage to the king at Kakh Golestan where the famous pearl and emerald-encrusted Peacock Throne is located. On those days, my father put on his black robe, a gold embroidered hat reminiscent of the ones worn by Eastern Orthodox clergy, and a white silk scarf over his right shoulder showing eleven golden chevrons to indicate his rank in the judicial system.

My father was proud of his status and of his genetic heritage, and he wanted to father many children. At the same time he felt his responsibility ended where emotional involvement began. He did not remember our ages and often had to ask which grade we were in at school. For the most part, he believed in the abilities and resourcefulness of my sister and me, firmly convinced we would do well regardless of the paths we chose in life. Though he did not openly show tenderness or exhibit affection toward me, I overheard him saying good things on many occasions to his friend about me.

For a long time I believed he was incapable of showing any open affection. But when my sister Mariam was born, his distant attitude softened considerably. He held Mariam in his arms, talked to her in a soothing voice, and sang to her frequently.

When Mariam was just a few months old, I heard my father coo to her and speak baby-talk for the first time. He turned to me and pointed to a purplish birthmark on Mariam's upper lip.

"See Ba Ba Jan," he said. "My little flower has a rosebud on her lip. If she ever gets lost, I can easily find her."

He held her to his chest and began to sing. Mariam's birth gave our family the warmth and cohesiveness we suspected but never knew for sure was missing.

But, my father's negative opinion about my half-brother Manuchehr never changed. My father did not think him to be intelligent or ambitious enough to do much with his life. Manuchehr was born into a temporary marriage or *sigheh* as it is referred to under Islamic law, which allows men to have as many wives as they wish by simply declaring, "I marry you, I marry you, I marry you," and as easily divorce a woman by declaring "I divorce you, I divorce you, I divorce you."

Manuchehr was born in 1929 at the height of the Reza Shah's secular regime. Manuchehr was the byproduct of a marriage of convenience. His mother was a farmer's daughter from a village close to Tehran. She never visited, and my father only half-heartedly accepted his new son.

Manuchehr had his own room where he ate alone, slept alone, and where he did his homework in the shadows cast by the weak light of a kerosene lamp. He spent a good deal of time in the alleys and did not do well at school.

My father's deep resentment of Manuchehr made it difficult for all of us, especially for my mother who wanted to care for him as her own. I never heard my father say one good thing about him, and my mother as intermediary could neither please Manuchehr nor my father no matter how hard she tried. The slow-burning grudge was too powerful to settle. Manuchehr and my father fought a lot. Sometimes my father beat him with a belt. I was sad and felt helpless to see him singled out like that.

With the different and unfair treatment by my father, I understood Manuchehr's bitterness toward my sister and me and felt the increasing emotional distance between us.

Manuchehr finished public high school and served two years as a conscript in the air force. Afterward, he was employed by the Iranian Oil Company and transferred to Abadan's oil refineries, which were still under British control. Manuchehr grew up to look like my father, with the same facial features and same green eyes, but unlike my father, he kept his hair and did not gain weight. With his Douglas Fairbanks mustache, freckled face, and green eyes, he looked handsome and happy in the pictures he would send to us from Abadan. In his early twenties, he married a high-maintenance girl whose family claimed to be the descendants of the Qajar Dynasty, the succession of Persian leadership from 1794 to 1925. Manuchehr's marriage, unlike the Qajar's lengthy dynasty, lasted just a couple of months. His second wife, a nice woman named Forozandeh, died young from breast cancer.

Years later and long after I had left the country, I was deeply immersed one evening studying in my home in Western New York when suddenly Forozandeh's image came to mind. The thought of her was so unusual and so out of context that I wrote the date and the time of the vision in the margin of the book I was reading. I learned a few days later, when speaking with my mother on the phone, how accurately the timing of my vision coincided with the exact time of Forozandeh's death.

Manuchehr, like me, does not believe in organized religion. There is no way he would say what I experienced qualified as a "divine vision." He would call it coincidence. I would disagree. There is a connectedness in the universe beyond the phenomenal world. I've seen it first-hand through my experiences and in my travels. I've touched this thread and felt it resonate with vibrations from around the world.

I tell Manuchehr, "These connections are real."
"I don't see it," he answers.
And I laugh because he reminds me so much of my father.

3. A BUSY BOY IN THE BAZAAR

I was born and lived until my early teens in the same small house in the southern part of Tehran among narrow alleys housing a cross-section of society. Mine was a neighborhood of shop-keepers, merchants, teachers, and civil servants.

In our neighborhood, I played with the son of a milkman, a black boy whose great grandfather had been a slave. Very few slaves were brought to Persia during this shameful era; none of their descendents was treated with prejudice or discrimination. Ali was soft-spoken, a meek kid with small ears. He lived across from us with his parents and grandparents in two rented rooms. His father left very early in the morning to deliver milk, which he carried in a metal container on the back of his bicycle.

Another playmate was Reza, a clumsy cross-eyed boy. Even though he was big, he was teased for his awkwardness and funny walk. His father was a heavy man who sold leeches as a blood-letting cure-all. Reza was the only boy among a few older sisters; the oldest one would have been a very pretty girl if not for the ravages of small pox scars.

There were few educated families like ours in the neighborhood. I knew I was different but did not know why. I understood my father was different from the other fathers, the way he dressed in European style, the respect and deference he received from others, and when he went to greet the king in his judicial robe, people watched him with awe. He did not associate with anyone in the neighborhood, and I heard on many occasions that he was in a higher social and intellectual class than others.

Our home had four rooms and a small yard with a water reservoir filled by a manual water pump. The kitchen was a dark, sunken room demanding a deep bow to allow for entrance. My mother did the cooking by kerosene, so the crude fireplace was rarely used. The floor of the corner room was covered by a thin, well-worn kilim, woven Persian carpets, with traces of blue flowers now faded with age. To keep away the relentless heat of summer and the harsh cold of winter, the door was kept closed, leaving the room in semi-darkness most of the time. It is into this darkness that one of my earliest memories takes me:

Lying in a hammock, my eyes grow heavy, and the world hazes over and folds in on itself. The breeze from the rhythmic swaying caresses my warm skin. The edges of the brown, crooked rafters that support the straw ceiling begin to fade away. The animated images that my mind has conjured from the curving slopes of the white-washed walls continue their story-telling into my dream as I fall asleep. I dream of a white cloud in a soft blue sky. The pigeons and the one -legged stork are high up in the tree. As I hear the diminishing screeching sound of the hammock, my heavy eyes open slightly to discern the crude, heavy metal nail in the corner to which the hammock rope is attached. I am surrounded by darkness. I am alone.

Most yards in our area were not big enough for trees or bushes, but the larger homes such as our neighbor's often had sizable orchards. A low wall separated our houses and allowed a full view of the sycamore and oak trees where I would spend hours at a time watching the birds come and go. A stork with its nest high in a tree fascinated me. I knew with his majestic wing span, he had the freedom to fly anywhere. I imagined him flying over the highlands and valleys with brilliant sunshine and roaring rivers along the way. At sunset, I was comforted when I saw him back in his nest. The thought of his daily adventures warmed my heart.

When I wasn't bird-watching, I was active and underfoot. I must have been around three or four and full of energy when my mother sent me to a neighbor's home in order to get me out of her hair. She called me over and asked me to run next door to pick up a box of *begir va benshan*, a term that, unbeknownst to me, translated literally as, "keep him occupied for a while."

Eager to pick up this mysterious "box," I happily dashed off to see Sedigheh, our neighbor, who lived in a large house with her parents. The house had an elaborate, heavy door opening onto a round patio with a reservoir of water at its center. This was a common feature in traditional Persian homes where guests could pause before entering the inner sanctum.

I played with the kids and joined them in picking grapes from the small rows of vines in the yard. I forgot all about the mysterious *begir va benshan* box, which wasn't mentioned again until the next time I got too hyper and my mother needed a break.

Sedigheh's merchant father, Haj Agha, lived on one side of the building with his wife, and Sadigheh with her husband and two kids lived on the other. Owning a shop in the Bazaar was a valuable possession which remained in the family through inheritance by the sons or marriage through the daughters.

Historically, the Bazaar had always played a central role in Iranian society and especially in the lives of those in Southern Tehran. As the commercial heart of the nation it pulsated with economic, social, and religious activity. Here, it was impossible to ignore the influence of Islam; one could not escape the blaring speakers bellowing out the words of the Koran or the mullahs who preached from the mosques on every corner. The bazaar was a maze of narrow alleys covered by domed roofs with an opening at the top to allow a well-delineated shaft of bright sunlight to penetrate the darkness. It was a kaleidoscopic sea of humanity and a feast for the eyes.

Porters moved merchandise in and out of the bazaar among the traffic of men, women, children, donkeys, bicycles, and mopeds. Men carried hookah in one hand and in the other, trays full of delicately balanced glasses of hot tea held high to avoid collisions. On their heads, some carried trays full of chelo-kabob (rice and kabob) under metallic covers to keep the food warm. Beggars flaunted their assortment of afflictions in the form of congenital and acquired diseases, competing for the sympathies and donations of passers-by.

Each section of the bazaar was dominated by a specialty. The section for jewelers displayed a glittering array of gold and diamonds in brightly-lit windows.

Around the corner, among colorful heaps of Persian rugs, the carpet-seller sat, somber and serious, busy with his abacus and prayer beads.

The next bend took me to the world of herbs and dry foods, with vivid displays of saffron turmeric, cumin, ginger, cinnamon, and coriander, all heaped in colorful mountains on deep wooden trays.

From blocks away I could hear the rhythmic poundings of the silversmiths and other metal workers. There were sections for clothing, leather goods, vegetables, fruits, and meat. For the thirsty, a man sold water, which he carried in an animal hide on his shoulder and dispensed in a metallic bowl engraved with religious verses.

Just beyond the bustle of the bazaar, our neighborhood was a hodgepodge of different-sized and styled houses situated throughout a maze of narrow alleys. At the middle of each alley was an open, shallow channel. It was dry and full of debris most of the time except when the district received its allocated supply of water. During the designated night for the water allocation, the whole neighborhood, hurricane-lamps in hand, would help supervise the diversion of the water to their own covered reservoirs. For us kids, this was one of the more exciting events. Staying up until the early hours of the morning, going in and out of the houses under the opaque light of the hand-held lamps, participating in building dams to divert the water to one house and destroying other dams to reroute the water to another, was exhilarating. In the covered reservoir, deposits sank down in the muddy water leaving the top clear and relatively potable. Still, such water was a major source of infectious diseases from all sorts of bacteria and was a major cause of mortality, especially among children. Iran had one of the highest infant mortality rates in the world, and the adults, with an average life span of fifty years, did not fare much better.

Water was and remains a most precious commodity, one that could someday replace oil as a major source of conflict among the nations in the region. The most significant source of water in Iran came through a series of interconnected wells called Ghanat. This labor-intensive and ancient irrigation system managed to squeeze out the last drop of underground water that the parched land had to give. One could better appreciate the extent of such an irrigation system by flying over the country and observing the wells forming the vast Ghanat system.

The digging of such wells was done in much the same way as it had been done thousands of years ago. The soil was transported by a hand-stitched, cow-hide sack, which dangled from a crude rope wrapped around a wooden-square-frame. This frame rotated around a wooden axis supported by a bifurcated tree stump in each side. The task was performed by two men: one person at the bottom of the well digging and filling the sack, the other using his hands and legs to rotate the frame and lift up the sack full of dirt. Generation after generation, perhaps millions of men, had endured the same task over and over again. Bound to this wheel, they seemed resigned to their destiny. I felt sorry for them and wished everyone could be more like my long-legged storks, flying free and coming home, better off at the end of the day than they were at the beginning.

When I was five years old, I started school at the local kindergarten run by a blind man affectionately called Baba Noghli. (*Noghle* is a candy served on auspicious occasions.) A jolly, high-spirited middle-aged man, he came from an aristocratic family. Rumor had it that he had gone blind because of syphilis. We loved him because he gave us candy nearly every day. His wife, on the other hand, a strict disciplinarian, chased us with a stick. In the afternoons at school, we took naps and fell asleep to the delicious odor of *compote de pomme* and other stewed fruits. The next two years passed in a blissful blur of naps and candy.

Near the end of the third grade and close to summer vacation, one day Baba Noghli told me to go home.

I asked, "Why? What's wrong?"

Baba Noghli was silent.

"Did I do something bad?" I asked.

He repeated, "Go home," then turned around and left it at that.

I was seven-years-old and had no idea what was going on. As I rounded the bend and still a few houses away from my own, I smelled the pleasant aroma of the cooking, baking, and heard noisy chatter coming from our yard. Opening the door, I was surprised to see my aunts and uncles and cousins standing in the middle of the yard talking in raised voices as Persians so often do. As I walked in, the chatter stopped. Deciding on an optimistic approach, I anticipated a joyous occasion, maybe even a surprise party or something. But, when Mr. Shoa the barber arrived, fear rose in my throat, and a thump of dread pounded in my gut. I knew that in addition to cutting hair, Mr. Shoa was also the man who performed ritual circumcisions.

Mr. Shoa was in his middle fifties. He had scanty fluffs of poorly Hanna-dyed hair wisping around his pudgy face and down to his fleshy chin. His light green eyes were flat and expressionless.

Recognizing my apprehension, I was showered with conciliatory words and assurances that before I knew it, it would all be over. My eighteen-year-old uncle Mahmood grabbed me in a vice-like grip that nearly collapsed my lungs and left me little room to breathe. He locked my wrists under my knees and pried my legs apart from behind with his elbows. I struggled and pleaded, begging to be released, but I might as well have begged for sympathy from a stone wall.

The men in the room, my uncle included, encircled me. Mr. Shoa slid a menacing white-handled razor from his creased leather bag. The slanting afternoon light reflected against the steel blade as he wiped it carefully, almost lovingly, with alcohol. Another pair of hands locked onto my wrists and a third pair held my head as I thrashed around. With my pants down, I closed my eyes. I felt a searing pain and heard the shouts of *"Tammam shod! Tammam shod,"* "It is over! It is over!" from the men. Through a hazy curtain of tears, I saw the blood-soaked sheet under me and the blue flame of the burning alcohol-soaked cotton balls as Mr. Shoa prepared the bandages to prevent further bleeding.

My mother kept me home from school for a few days and helped me tie a thin towel around my waist. When not writhing in bed, wondering if I might die at any minute, I winced my way around the house like an old man trudging through mud. My mother's home-made cookies nearly made the experience worthwhile, although it certainly didn't qualify as a ritual I'd care to repeat.

As if that weren't enough, I soon encountered the ritual of blood-letting. The next summer, I found myself plagued by a curious skin rash. I woke up one day with a few red spots on my neck and shoulders. Two days later I looked like I'd been assaulted by a few thousand venomous scorpions. My arms turned blotchy, and enough of my skin flaked off to make me wonder if I might molt away to nothing and disappear forever. I couldn't sleep at night and begged Allah to forgive me for whatever transgression had brought about such vindictive retribution. With no relief in sight and with Allah mysteriously quiet about the burning rash, I took matters into my own hands by scrubbing myself to painful ecstasy from top to bottom with a pumice stone. One day, my mother escorted a strange woman into the house in order to treat me by blood-letting. The woman pulled out a razor blade, similar to the kind my father used, from a small black case. Turning me around by my shoulders, she slid the blade down my back as I shrieked and my mother ordered me to stand still.

"This will cure your rash," the woman said as she applied a suction cup to draw more blood.

Although only eight-years-old, it occurred to me as I stood there bleeding in the living room, that in my family, the cures seemed to hurt at least as much as the diseases.

After a few days of rest, it was back to the safe haven of school.

Although we found ways to have fun, we didn't have formal recreational facilities at our school. Our recreational centers were the alleys and the streets where I played with the working class kids. The more well-educated Persians such as my parents lived in the northern section of town. It was my father's lack of sensitivity about this issue that kept us in a neighborhood where we clearly did not belong.

Here, the kids did not use their given names but instead went by their street nicknames. In our neighborhood, we had kids with names like Akbar Dilang ("uncoordinatedly tall"), Reza Shooli ("jelly-like"), Ahmad Ghoosi ("humpback"), "Naghi Booghi ("horny voice"), and Hussein Kaftary ("pigeon") whose brother owned a bunch of domesticated pigeons.

Among the boys I hung around, very few had a bike or a ball or a toy. Games revolved around the ingenuity of the kids. For entertainment, we picked up some kid's hat or swiped one off a passerby and passed it back and forth as our victim jumped and lunged for it to our unending delight.

Rolling an iron hoop with a stick in the alleys with a gang of boys was a highlight of most days. Among our gang, some had cycle rims, a couple had barrel bands, and a few others had nothing at all to roll. This last unfortunate group kept running with us with their imaginary hoops in one hand, holding up their flimsy pajama bottoms with the other.

The purchase of my own first rim was my first real thrill. I frequently washed and cleaned the rim as if it were a shiny sports car. I parked it safely in our yard and enjoyed the surge of pleasure I got from looking at it.

After we'd exhausted the possibilities of rolling a metal rim through the streets, a lack of opportunity combined with our excessive energy found its outlet in an ongoing war between us and the Dooroshkeh drivers.

In the early Forties, Tehran had few buses. The dominant mode of getting around town came in the form of the horse-drawn carriages called a Dooroshkeh. For kids the challenge of hitching a free ride on the back of the Dooroshkeh was irresistible. The trick was to jump on without attracting the attention of the drivers who would delight in whipping us like crazy if we were caught. This hostility reached its height during the month of Ramadan when the rhythm of daily life changed. During this month, people got up before dawn, ate a light meal called *sahari*, and prayed shortly after when the Muazzin broke the silence of the night. The next meal after each day of fasting would be at sunset, often followed by religious gatherings in homes or mosques. During Ramadan, people stayed up much later at night, and the streets remained busy with a lot more traffic. Late in such evenings, we kids gathered in strategic locations in the streets with an ample supply of cut-up watermelon rinds as ammunition to take revenge against the carriage drivers. I can't say for sure what role such juvenile behavior played in my growing love for adventure, but you haven't lived until you've thrown watermelon rinds at unsuspecting carriage drivers in the middle of the night.

Almost as much fun were the annual picnics with my aunt and cousins. We rode along together in an old carriage usually used for hauling bricks. Choosing one of the better horses for the occasion and covering the flat carriage with carpet, we filled the middle with

pots and pans, cooked and uncooked food, and sat along the edge
of the carriage with our feet dangling as we traveled through the
city's dusty streets. There was a lot of pushing and shoving among
the kids to get the best seat next to the driver, which was always a
guaranteed pleasant spot unless the horse happened to be especially
flatulent that day.

We arrived hours later in the neighboring village at the outskirts
of town where we stretched out our carpet by the brook and started
the food preparation and tea-making rituals for the evening meal.
After dinner everyone tried to sleep for a few hours. We began our
long walk in the early morning toward "Bee Bee Shahrbanoo," a
humble building with a blue dome and minarets located at the
heart of the mountain. The pilgrims treated it like any other
religious site, donating, praying, lighting candles and demanding
miracles and cures for their various illnesses. I loved the walk up
the gentle mountain. The sky full of stars. The cool fresh breeze.
And the soft lights of the hurricane-lamp that turned the ocher
path into a meandering, golden and glowing road up the steep hill
ahead.

Back home, we'd fall asleep, exhausted. Energized the next day
and having forgotten about the serenity of the mountain, we set
out into the streets to wreak as much havoc as we could get away
with.

Mischievous behavior was a major source of our entertainment
and laughter in those days. Religious gatherings during the month
of Ramadan provided the ideal milieu for such activities. When
Ramadan coincided with summer, such religious gathering were
held outdoors, usually in the houses of the well to do Bazaaries.
Haj Agh Reza was a wealthy merchant who lived around the corner
from us and held regular religious services.

Sometimes the kids would sneak in to watch the sacred
ceremonies. Although still very young, I rebelled against what
I considered to be the phoniness of these religious rituals.
Occasionally, though, I found unique ways to enjoy the experience.

The sun disappears behind the houses in a trail of purple, dissolving into a dark blue. Darkness spreads fast, and the Muazzin calls for the evening prayer. Dim lights began to turn on here and there as folks prepare to break their fast.

I'm twelve years old, and Akbar Dillang, Naghi Booghy and I, are hiding a few houses away from Haj Agha Reza's house waiting for his guests to arrive.

The stifling heat has abated, and a cool breeze appeases our impatience. The last roaming stray dogs nose through the piles of garbage collecting against the alley walls. The alley in front of the entrance of Haj Agha Reza's home shows the circular traces of the long-handled broom still moist by splashed water to keep down the dust. The dim light at the end of the cement poles flickers yellow over the increasing traffic of men and veiled women heading toward the gathering. We blend in, and enter the cobblestone hall leading to the yard with a large rectangular water reservoir at its center. We take our shoes off and place them neatly in rows among hundreds of others and sit cross-legged on the yard's carpeted floor. The atmosphere is oppressive and somber. There is not a happy face in the crowd. The silence is interrupted by a litany of "salam alycom" greetings. Men keep fiddling with their prayer beads.

There is a single chair for the Mullah close to a short curtain separating the women's prayer section from the men's.

During the course of the evening, several mullahs appear. Each launches one at a time into a sermon for ten or fifteen minutes about the basic tenets of religion. Each homily begins somber and slow. Soon after however, the Mullahs rev up into more emotional issues, focusing on martyrdom and the persecution of the Shiite leader Imam Hussein at the hands of the cruel Sunni leaders Yazid, Shemre and Abu Bakr. The audience responds with cries and moans and self-flagellation as if hearing for the first time this shocking news from fourteen-hundred years ago. The gradual charging of the emotions gathers more speed, reaching its crescendo at the end when the lights are turned off. In the near-darkness, the Mullah describes, with grand embellishments, the gory details of the massacre of the seventy-two person entourage of Imam Hussein. He works the crowd into a frenzy. His audience responds by upping the ante and going at least a couple octaves higher. I sit in the dark with my eyes wide open, observing the bizarre theatricality of the scene. I see the transparency of their beliefs behind the façade of their clumsy acting.

It is at the height of the crying and moaning that my friends and I make our move and tip-toe out to where the men have lined up their shoes. Stifling our giggles behind our hands, we quietly gather and dump as many of the men's single shoes as we can into the pool.

Then we dash off behind some bushes near the entry way to watch the scene. The search for the missing shoes at the end of the service creates pandemonium with shouted accusations and vociferous arguments. Since most men wear similar shoes, with limited colors and styles, the claim on each other's remaining shoe is made even more earnest. We watch from behind the bushes and laugh until we think we'll die.

Some of the duped men hop on one foot, cursing; others give and receive piggyback rides. A few simply sit down where they are as if waiting for their missing shoes to return by magic.

4. BUSTLING IN THE BACK ALLEYS

While we were playing practical jokes, the adults were busy drinking tea. The ritual of tea-making, tea-drinking, and gathering around the samovar were essential elements in Persian life.

Tea was served for social occasions, for breakfast, and after each meal. Every home, no matter how humble, had a samovar and went through the same ritual: First hot charcoal was prepared in a device called an *ateshgardan*, literally a "mover of the fire." This was a grapefruit-size gadget made of thin wire in which charcoal turns red hot by being rotated in the air. I liked to perform this task of turning. It reminded me of the catapulting power of the fire-throwers in medieval battles attempting to overtake an impenetrable castle. After rotating the charcoal, I placed it in the cylindrical container of the samovar to heat the water in its reservoir. Tea was served in small glass containers on an intricately-decorated china saucer and consumed with a solid lump of sugar, which was placed in the corner of the mouth to last the full glass.

Along with tea, the other Iranian staple was bread, especially *nane sangak*, or "pebble bread," consumed with cheese for breakfast.

One of my responsibilities before going to school was to purchase bread and cheese, to be used fresh daily. The bakery had a blue tiled arched-entry with an arabesque design. The cashier sat in the doorway and ushered customers into a large, dark room where people waited their turn to receive bread. The baking was a two-man operation. A man named *Shatter* wore a white apron and wielded his long-handled paddle like a warrior with a broadsword. He picked up the dough from a large wooden reservoir, placed it over the rectangular surface of the paddle with a long handle, and flattened it out. He moved with rhythmic predictability and the precision of a dancer. He took short and long steps, stretching on his toes to the right and left before delivering the dough into the maw of the large gas oven. His movements had the artistic elements evocative of the Persian folk dance, called *shatery*. Shatter was the nobler of the two bakers. He seldom looked at the customers and rarely haggled with them.

His partner was king of the dark bakery cave. He removed the fresh bread with the help of metallic rods, long as a devil's pitchfork, and distributed it to the waiting customers. The trick for us was to let him know we were there and what place we held in the throng of customers. Since I was a kid, I had to work twice as hard and shout twice as loud to make my presence known. I did as others did, shouting, "Salam alaycom!" over and over to get the baker's attention. Each customer made a mental note of the order in which every other customer had arrived, and constant fights erupted over who was ahead of whom. I grew accustomed to the pushing and jostling and did my best to avoid being trampled.

One day I walked into the bakery just as a fight broke out. Two men, Akbar and Hassan, had apparently arrived in the store at the exact same time and couldn't resolve who should be allowed to place his order first. Akbar, although the smaller of the two men, aggressively asserted his priority and poked Hassan in the chest with his stubby finger, claiming that not only had he arrived first but that Hassan had sprung from questionable parentage and had the brains of a donkey. Hassan, stunned at the smaller man's explosive hostility, took a step back to gather himself before informing Akbar that not only were his parents of *superior* moral character, but that his brother Ahmed just got a job as a supervisor in the same factory where Akbar worked. "One word from me," Hassan hissed to Akbar, "and you're fired and your family will starve in the streets." Akbar stepped aside, and Hassan walked to the front to receive his order as the other men laughed and cheered.

When my turn came, the quarreling men had gone, and I left with my hot bread wrapped in a towel and went to Said Ali Agha's store next door to buy cheese.

Said Ali Agha wore thick eyeglasses. I often wondered how he didn't pitch forward from the weight. I imagined he must be able to see great distances with those powerful lenses. Sometimes my mother made spinach stew, which was one of my favorites. When she didn't add enough little meatballs, I would poke around for more, joking to her that I needed Said Ali Agha's glasses to find the meatballs, and my mother would laugh.

As I entered Said Ali Agha's shop, I wished him a good day and placed my order. I hoped his glasses wouldn't fall into the briny bath from which he drew the cheese with is hennaed hand.

Although still early in the morning, the steamy shop of the *Kaleh Pacheh* was already crowded with laborers having their breakfast around the dilapidated tin-covered tables and benches. Here, they cooked the heads and hooves of lambs and sold the assorted internal organs of sheep.

I passed by a group of men. They wore tattered clothes and stood or squatted around the shops hoping for work as a day laborer.

I approached the *Zoor Khaneh*, or "House of Strength," where some men did their daily physical activities and body-building. As I got near, I heard the percussion of drums and the singing of the impresario reciting the poetry of Ferdowsi, the great 10th century Persian poet. I was intrigued by the house's low entrance door. The door, I'd been told, had been built low on purpose in order to make each person who entered bow to Imam Ali, the symbol of strength in Islam, whose picture hung on the opposite wall. A thick curtain guarded the entrance door and piqued my curiosity. I hoped for a glance of the inside as I passed but had no such luck. From overheard stories, I tried to piece together what must be happening behind the curtain. I imagined a house filled with tattooed men in a round pit. They performed various exercises and wore leather pants extending to mid-calf. They swung wooden clubs in the air, did push-ups, and whirled around, arms extended, over and over again. Hearing the ringing of the bell by the impresario, I surmised that someone had dominated in wrestling or had triumphed in a contest of push-ups or weightlifting.

Wrestling was a traditional sport among Persians. Historically, they performed well in the international arena. A young man by the name of Takhti, who was a member of the same Zoor-Khaneh, won an Olympic gold medal. His exceptional talent and reputation as a wrestler plus his political views against the Shah's regime had made him popular. But when he refused to shake hands with the Shah and died soon after from an apparent suicide, rumors started springing up, and he went from champion wrestler to national folk hero.

The streets and alleys of Southern Tehran were a hodgepodge of people creating a wide way of life out of a narrow lot. Different seasons, different days of the week, and different hours of the day, brought different characters and various scenes to the back alleys of Southern Tehran. One could predict the time of day or time of year by listening to the cries of whichever vendor happened to be passing by.

The vendors filled the streets and sold bin after bin of herbs, spices, fruits, vegetables, salt, sugar, fabrics, cooking pots, and charcoal.

Contrary to popular misconceptions, winters in Tehran were quite cold and often saw significant snow accumulation. I once had a bad enough case of frostbite on my toes to be treated with the traditional home remedy of mashed boiled turnips that were applied systematically to my burning feet for weeks. It was a messy process, and the benefits were questionable, although it wasn't as bad as the blood-letting for my skin rashes.

Harsh prolonged winters drew Iranians inside their homes and around Korsi to share its warmth. This contraption consisted of a low square table covered with a very large comforter extending on four sides. Folks sat around it on mattresses and leaned back against cushions for support. A brazier containing smoldering balls of ground-up charcoals that was placed under it, provided the heat they shared.

In the long winter nights, korsi served as the centerpiece of family activities. People sat around to converse, socialize, read, or just doze off. Children did their homework around the korsi, and the family ate dinners on its flat surface.

The charcoal balls were prepared in the fall. Vendors with their donkeys or camels delivered the powdery black charcoal, which we mixed in large containers of water and placed in orange-sized balls outside to dry in the sun. I loved to get my hands into the gooey black stuff and make the little charcoal balls. At the end of the day, I had fun looking in the mirror at my face, which was always black with ash.

To combat heavy snow falls, men carried wooden shovels for clearing snow from the flat rooftops of precariously leaning homes. The newspapers routinely reported of substantial mortality as the result of roof collapses during the winter time. Although people think of Iran as an enormous desert, nothing could be further from the truth. Iran hosts a range of temperatures and topographies from flat arid stretches to jagged snow-capped mountains to lush areas of vibrant verdancy.

As varied as the land itself, the accents of the vendors ran an equally impressive range. Some sang melodically; others screeched. Some vendors carried their produce on their backs, others on trays on their heads, and still others by donkey or by the more modern push carts. During the hot summer days, the Ice Man carried muddy chunks of ice on a donkey, selling bricks of ice door to door under the blazing sun, watching his worldly belongings melting away. I never knew what debris or impurity I might find in a purchased chunk of ice, and I picked up the habit of haggling to go after the cleanest, clearest pieces.

My favorite of the vendors was the man who carried a large metallic box on his back. The box was painted in a wild assortment of colors and had two openings to look through. The man was called Shahre Farangi or "Foreign City." Anything that had a hint of foreignness to it, anything that took the imagination into the world beyond, was appealing to me. For a penny, we looked through one of the two openings while the man rotated a crudely cut and poorly pasted hodgepodge of pictures past the eye hole. As he spun the picture wheel, he narrated a story about each passing scene. Sometimes he didn't get the story to match up exactly with the rotating pictures. When that happened, I interrupted him, asking where was this or that picture he was talking about. I told him, "The pictures aren't right. You need to fix your story."

I'm glued to the round opening. I've got my hands cupped around my eyes to prevent the bright sun from diminishing the weak lighting of my fantasy world. I'm looking at a completely empty screen.

The storyteller says, "Here is the white horse of Rostam, grazing in the lush greenery along the Sabalan range."

I shout, "Hey! I see no horse, no grass, and no mountain."

The man looks down. He sees I'm right. The screen is blank. He doesn't miss a beat. He says, "The horse has eaten the grass."

"What about the horse?" I shout back, my eyes still riveted to the opening.

The man replies, "There is no more grass so the horse has gone away."

This is my movie theater and my circus in one. I purchase my popcorn, which we call choce-a-phil, literally meaning, "the elephant's fart," from a deformed man, always seated like a permanent fixture on the way to my grandmother's home. He is leprous with a leonine face.

I am getting a sense of other worlds, that there is more out there beyond the desperate men in dusty alleys. I am preoccupied with my soaring imaginative fantasy of highlands and valleys where my birds and the stork are taking me. I am still a child, but something stirs in me. It's more than a simple longing. It's a knowledge, a knowledge that my spirit isn't meant to sit still. And at the same time, the pageantry of life and its transparency that is displayed so openly out in the streets and the alleys of Tehran fascinates me.

In the streets, on my way home, repair men and artisans announced their skill in fixing any broken item a person might have. One man specialized in fixing broken china. He drilled holes in each piece with his primitive drill. He kept the pieces together with small metallic clips. He accepted a broken teapot from an old woman. I watched as he performed his magic. He handed her the teapot, which she took from him with a smile. A few minutes later, she was running past me back toward the repair man. She had the teapot clamped in both hands. Water had spewed all over her through its jagged, leaking seams.

I laughed and passed by *panbeh zan,* or "the cotton shredder." His task was to separate the matted cotton of old mattresses into a fluffier form for new ones.

I stopped to watch him work. His tool of the trade was a strange, cumbersome instrument. It looked like a cross between a huge bow and a single-stringed harp. Curved at the ends, the wooden device was about three inches thick and four feet long. A thick string made of animal gut connected the two curved ends. Squatting, the man vibrated the string against the heap of matted cottons with a wooden pestle causing the thousands of particles to separate. Most landed on him, and as I watched, he turned into a fluffy, new-born bird.

In addition to the merchants and artisans, a group of entertainers often passed through the district. They played music in the alleys to inform their presence, and when paid enough, would perform privately in people's backyards.

The ensemble of our neighborhood was a quartet that comprised a singer and his red-jacketed pet monkey, a violinist, a percussionist, and a man who played the *kmancheh*, an instrument that resembled a small, bottom-heavy cello. The leader disguised his long hair under a fedora and let it loose when he performed. He had a glass eye, a gaunt face, and an effeminate walk. We called him "Akram Khanoum," a title used for ladies.

Weddings varied according to the financial strength or social status of the families. Big and showy wedding festivities were important to Iranians. A bride's dowry was carried into her future home in a conspicuous way, as it was in the wedding of Effat, the daughter of Haj Aghas, our next door neighbor.

The air was filled with smoke from the wild rue burning in a golden brazier held by a woman in a colorful chador. On the floor of the dusty alley were at least twenty round boards in a row covered with white cloth and filled with household necessities ready to be transferred to the future home of the bride.

The musicians were hard at work. The glass-eyed singer was at the pitch of his song, while his monkey reached out for the *noghle* (sugar coated almonds) that were customarily thrown over the dowry in order to sweeten the marriage.

Aziz Katchal ("Azziz the Bald"), a witty porter known in the district for his jokes and pleasantries, carried the first tray on his head and began the procession with his exaggerated hip and hand movements preserved for such happy occasions. The others followed. As the procession of the porters, musicians, and children proceeded toward the future home of the bride, doors opened and the neighborhood men and women took full inventory of the dowry, whispering about the quality and relative opulence of each gift.

In the evening, a formal ceremony was held in the garden. The large water reservoir at the center of the garden was boarded and covered with carpets to serve as center stage for entertainment. Besides the singing and seductively-dancing women, there were live performances and sitcoms, mostly revolving around a main protagonist with a blackface. Full of wisecracks and humor, he represented the underdog and was invariably the star of the show and much loved by the audience.

From the rooftop, my cousin Parviz and I, both of us eleven-years-old, watched the entertainment, which started after sun down. We were in fifth grade at the time and were still learning to combine our energy with our ingenuity to pull pranks on unsuspecting adults.

The garden was crowded with men sitting around the yard behind tables filled with fruits and cakes. Parviz pointed out a guest sitting in front of a row of flowering pots. The guest sported a conspicuous gray hat of Persian lamb. When he removed his hat and left it under his chair to have dinner inside, Parviz looked at me with that special smirk that told me what he had in mind. We ran down, quickly removed one of the geraniums from its clay pot, and placed it in the hat with all its roots and soil. At the last minute we added some leftover tea to keep it moist and placed the hat back under the seat. We then returned to our strategic location on the rooftop to watch.

Soon we forgot our mischievous behavior, absorbed as we were by the seductive dancing women who performed well past midnight. For some time I was preoccupied with the thought of the female dancer. The feeling was different, new, and not specifically sexual but accompanied by a strong desire just to be near her. Thinking about her was soothing and pleasing, and I quickly forgot about the wedding guest and our prank with the hat.

In 1944-1945, third grade brought another challenge and another disappointment as I had to change schools. The school that housed the fourth grade, although new, had quickly become known for its heavy-handed discipline and liberal use of corporal punishment. I lived in a rough neighborhood with a lot of tough kids, so these disciplinary measures became a way of life.

The worst of the offenders were whipped almost daily on the soles of their bare feet in front of the entire student body. We gathered in the yard before classes started to watch the man in charge of punishment as he placed the looped rope around the bare feet of the student to keep him in a fixed position. He delivered hard lashes in the presence of teachers, the principal, and the loud cries of the student. The scene was horrible to watch. I stood behind others, refusing to see the barbarism but could not help hearing the agonizing shrieks and pleas of the student. For lesser offenses, hitting a student on the palm of his hand was a common punishment bestowed liberally to all.

The locally born and bred principal of the school who easily could have been mistaken for an English explorer on an African safari, raised terror in our hearts. A blond man, bordering on albino, he wore a two-piece suit and a bow tie. He had a safari hat and looked quite out of place in our school.

The quality of education was appalling, and the students, most of them very poor, came from families preoccupied with the misery of poverty and had little enthusiasm and no pressing desire to learn.

Soon after joining the school, I developed a louse infestation of my scalp and had to shave my head.

This was near the end of World War Two during which Allied forces had occupied Iran in order to provide material support for the Russian front against the Germans. A typhus epidemic was taking a huge toll in Eastern Europe especially in concentration camps and in the Middle East killing tens of thousands, among them and perhaps most famously, Anne Frank.

In Tehran, the dreaded disease began to spread virulently by infested lice brought from Eastern Europe. Though the ravages of the war per se were not as visible in Iran, its collateral damage in the form of epidemic diseases and a scarcity of food, medicine, and basic daily needs had a serious impact on people's lives.

All necessities were rationed during this time, and people routinely horded everything they could. When food grew scarce, people grew creative. Rumor had it that the strange taste of the bread was due to the addition of sawdust in the wake of a flour shortage.

My sickness during the epidemic of typhus started with an exploding headache. Looking at the light felt as if each ray had individually pierced my eyes with a needle. Soon I was covered with an extensive rash; some lesions became ulcerated and bled.

Out of fear of transmitting the disease to my sister and brother during my prolonged recovery, I was cared for at my grandmother's home. Half the time I was comatose, and from the other half I remember little other than the horrible taste of the bitter homemade remedies concocted by my grandmother. And, of course, there were the visits by our family physician Dr. Gangebakhsh. He did not have much to offer since antibiotics were not yet available, but his reassurance and caring presence remains a shining spot during those dark days. I believe his bedside manner, in conjunction with my grandmother's prayers, helped me considerably to overcome the dreaded illness.

I had been considered a goner by most who had observed me during my prolonged struggle with the disease. My brother Manuchehr told me later how terribly emaciated and skeleton-like I looked.

During summer recess from school, and finally on the mend, I was sent by my grandmother to my grandfather's brick factory at the periphery of town to get some money for her daily expenses. I hung around there all day and went back empty-handed over and over again.

While waiting, I picked up a customer's bicycle and rode around the block until his business finished. As short as the duration of such rides were, and as awkward as I was at riding an adult's bicycle, it gave me the greatest pleasure. I loved riding bikes. If someone had given me a bike and asked me to go to the other end of the world, I could have done it with joy. I forgot hunger and thirst as long as I was riding.

On a couple of occasions when the man who worked in my grandfather's office asked if I could ride his bike and pick up his lunch from quite a distance away, I happily agreed. His bike was a tall, heavy clunker with a horn and bells and other assorted paraphernalia. Since I was not tall enough to sit on the saddle, I had to pedal under the bar while tipping the bike away from me to maintain its balance. The man's wife had made some round meat patties along with potatoes and bread. She put the food in a metallic container with three separate compartments attached to a handle. On a bumpy, dusty road halfway through my trip, the dangling food container fell off the handle bars. Shocked, I watched, tangled in the bike, as patties of meat rolled along the dusty ground. I cleaned them as best as I could and delivered them on time. But the man never asked me to deliver his lunch again.

If no bike was available, I rode the donkeys waiting to be loaded with building material. I was frustrated by my inability to move the beasts no matter how much I kicked their sides or tried to imitate the sounds and calls made by their normal drivers. I had much better luck with the donkeys of the mullahs who also used them as the means of transport going from one home to another during *rozeh khani*, the readings of elegies and eulogies. On a few occasions, when I managed to ride their donkey while they were busy preaching in a home, their donkeys seemed feistier, more obedient, and a lot more fun to ride. I wondered if mullahs possessed the same skill in controlling the animals that they seemed to have on some people.

On the other side of the street from my grandfather's brick factory was the compound of the allied soldiers. The scattered structures were surrounded by a tall barbed-wire fence through which I could see the military barracks and the soldiers' baseball field. I was especially interested in watching Americans when they played baseball.

While I was separated from the soldiers by few feet, the barbed wire with its menacing sharp teeth seemed an insurmountable obstacle between our vastly different worlds. I was a mesmerized kid in a half-starved nation during the war, dusty and dirty from playing in and around the brick factory. The soldiers, safe and well-fed on their side of the fence, never acknowledged our existence. They were accustomed to the sight of poorly fed and poorly clothed children who swarmed around them like flies.

The Americans, with their green t-shirts and their ID tags dangling around their necks, were loud and full of laughter. They chewed gum and smoked fragrant cigarettes as they played baseball on the field of patchy grass.

Life over the next few years passed by relatively peacefully. I changed schools again, but even change had become routine. Days melted into weeks and into months, and I experienced an odd sense of calm followed by a nagging dread that perhaps my life's adventures had ended before I'd even grown old enough to appreciate them. Not that I longed for the idyllic days of whippings, blood-lettings, and ritual circumcision. But I sensed that life hadn't finished with me yet. I carried on with my daily regimen at school and at home, but a germ of an idea had planted itself in my head, an idea about growing into something beyond myself. The daily walk to and from school provided an opportunity to immerse myself into a fantasy world, finding myself on the stage as a singer warmly received by an applauding audience and next as a war hero charging on my horse against fleeing enemies.

I finished primary school without incident, but I noticed that the adventure bug and I were both growing steadily and rapidly and were getting closer and closer together all the time.

5. MY NEW HOME IN THE NORTH

For secondary education, I went to a much better public school a good thirty five-minute walk from my home. Because I went home for lunch, I usually made the trip four times a day. Students at the school were intelligent, advanced, and quite an improvement over the school I had left. In the beginning of the year, I became friends with a classmate who was, oddly enough, also named Fraydoon, and we spent a great deal of time together during the year. Fraydoon lived close to the school. I frequently visited him at his home after school hours to study or play. His tragic death the following year caused by a fall from the rooftop at his home came as a huge shock to me. His death hit me very hard. I spoke little about it. To what degree his death contributed to my depression over the following years is hard to know.

The year of his death, one of the worst years of my student life, was a mixture of frustration, humiliation, and a near total shattering of my self-confidence. A deep depression sapped me. I began to withdraw, and my grades suffered. My algebra teacher, unaware of how much the death of, a friend, a boy with my name, had devastated me, hounded me in every class. The teacher terrified me, and I froze in his presence. His relentless and persistent attempts to teach me math drove me to tears, which he ridiculed as an inherent weakness, calling me a *bacheh naneh*, or "Mamma's Boy." The term wounded me, and I despised him for it.

I failed not only algebra, but Arabic language as well.

I could not warm up to the Arabic language. This is the language of Koran used in non-Arab Muslim counties, as Latin in Christianity. The teacher was an obese, kind-hearted man who suffered from bad arthritis and shortness of breath. Although an older man, he was known for his sympathy toward orphans and those whose names had a prefix of "Saied," signifying they were descended from the prophet Muhammad. Grades in schools ranged from zeros to twenty. Any mark below ten was considered failure and required repeating the course.

During the final oral exam, after my miserable botching of an Arabic poem, when he declared my mark as seven, I said in a low voice, "Sir, I don't have a father." He declared my mark as nine. Encouraged, I pulled a second trick. "And Sir," I said, "I am also 'Saied.'" Looking at my name, a name that could not have been further away from Arabic origin, he reached for his cane.

Having failed two courses, I had to repeat the eighth grade. The failure in eighth grade was the most shameful event of my life. My ego took a major hit, but if anything, the failure and depression brought back my childhood fantasies of flight and fueled my growing ambition to travel the world and, ultimately, to succeed in life.

Gradually my interest and awareness of my surroundings began to improve. My depression lifted, and I turned from dwelling on the Fraydoon who had died to taking care of myself, the Fraydoon who had lived.

Around this time and when I was about sixteen, Iran began to emerge from its long and lethargic social hibernation. As I entered my teens and emerged from my own mental stagnation, the country began to take baby steps toward becoming a more progressive, modern society.

This veneer of modernization, imbued with the superficiality of western culture, was focused mostly in Tehran, the capital, and far less in the more remote parts of the country.

There were more cars, boutiques, and pretentious modern houses with marble facades. Many restaurants and nightclubs, all concentrated in the northern section of Tehran, sprang up practically overnight. The streets were flooded with Iranians dressed in the latest fashions and sporting hairdos, all with the excessive, conspicuous consumption of the nouveau riche.

To escape the relentless heat of summers, the well-to-do gathered in the lush green village of Tajrish on the hills of the Alborz peaks to promenade in the cool mountain air. This was the place to see and to be seen by others, to show off fashionable dresses or trendy, modern cars. The gathering was a Persian variation of strolling in the Champs-Elysée on a fine summer evening. Young men, well dipped in their favorite eau de cologne and boasting Cornell Wilde hair, smoked Winston or Lucky Strike cigarettes and watched the girls go by. Painted girls with stiff hairdos, platinum and silver streaked, showed off the latest fashions and nibbled on roasted popcorn, the must-have delicacy of the day.

All sorts of vendors set up shops on the sidewalks, not for necessities as in the alleys of the city, but for the sole sake of appeasing the burgeoning affluent Yuppies.

I walked with friends though "Sare Pol," as the location was called. I watched and listened, absorbing the sights, the smells, and the vibrations in the air.

Vendors sat on low stools, skillfully extracting fresh walnuts with the expertise of a squirrel and artfully piling the nuts one on top of the other on a metal tray in front of them.

A choir of vendors, young and old, melodic and sometimes outrageously out of tune, competed for the attention of passers-by.

I heard the cries of vendors shouting out the price of fruit, their voices overlapping with the cries of other men selling ice cream, fresh herbs, and grilled livers, hearts, and kidneys.

A young man sat in front of a flat board he had laid across a couple of bricks on the ground. He had placed three Pepsi bottles on the board. A hand-written sign leaning in front of his little display said, "Ali Akbar's Supermarket."

I stopped off like so many others did for roasted corn, cooked on hot charcoal, thrown into a pail of cold salty water, and voila, ready to eat.

A short drive from the crowded noisy Sare Pol, but still along the foothills of the Alborz mountain range, was another village called Niavaran, which was where my paternal grandmother had a summer cottage. I looked forward to spending time during the summer holidays at her cottage. I was in that awkward transitional period of my life, considered not a boy anymore but not yet a man either, watching with yearning the young lovers as they drove along the village's fields of strawberry and wheat.

My grandmother's modest summer cottage with its mud and straw walls had a small orchard with pomegranate, apple, and quince trees dwarfed by a towering mulberry tree at the center. Its imposing trunk was crisscrossed with scars, and its gnarled branches splayed out monstrously in every direction.

I walked through the precipitous cobble-stoned paths of the village, flanked by mud walls and brightly colored doors to the open wheat fields where the peasants worked around heaps of harvested wheat under the golden haze of the slanting sun. Their primitive farming tools were much the same as the ones used by their ancestors who had cultivated this ancient land for a millennium.

Barefoot men in coarse, colorless shirts turned brown by dust and sweat, wore baggy black cotton pants as they toiled under the hot sun. The better-off wore traditional foot gear called *giveh*, a leather or rubber-soled shoe with the upper part made from colorful, woven thread. The men's faces, bronzed from the sun, were topped with thick skull caps. Some secured their long-stemmed smoking pipes with a piece of cloth around their waists.

Women in their wonderfully colorful dresses, traditional scarves, and black pants worked alongside the men. The women, as they worked, secured their children to their backs with long strips of fabric.

I loved the panoramic view of the snow-capped mountains. From the cottage, I often looked out on the sparkling golden wheat as it was thrown in the air to separate it from the chaff. I could sit and stare for hours at the slow-moving white donkey as he circled around the heap of harvested wheat, threshing it with a harness attached to his back.

As the sun sank past the horizon and the golden rays changed to a dimmer rose-colored light, each family gathered around the fire on their own little patch of earth. Women stretched out their carpets, fed their babies, and prepared tea and dinner. As I passed among them, they called "Befarma! Befarma!" an invitation for me to share their meal.

On many occasions I witnessed their generosity in sharing with total strangers. If giving attests to the nobility of human character, to give when having so little spoke of a spiritual generosity beyond the materialistic world.

The ethereal beauty of a simple life, connectedness to nature, and harmony with what life had to offer, and accepting it with such serenity are some of the qualities that have impressed me most about the working and peasant classes of Iran. When I think of Iranians, this is what I always remember and treasure from the people of my old country.

By the time I was old enough to drive with my own perfumed dates through the bucolic moonlit Niavaran village, the fragrance of the strawberries and the panoramic view of the golden wheat fields had given away to a different but equally magical world. Iran was changing at a rapid pace.

Like the newly affluent young Iranians, my family was financially comfortable, but we were no match for the social-climbing and often corrupt upper crust of Iranian society. While most of those with my father's position and educational background who worked within the system had achieved considerably higher social and financial status, my father was content with the life that his salary as a judge provided and never mixed with the wheelers and dealers in a system that he believed was corrupt to its core.

Corruption so imbued the Iranian culture that those who did not partake in it were looked upon as odd. This degenerate characteristic of the upper class was a major source of concern and disappointment and was among the principal reasons that some of us in the younger generation wanted to leave the country.

It took a lot of cajoling from my family to convince my father to leave the undesirable neighborhood of the South where I grew up and move to the lower level of a spacious two-story brick house in the northern part of the city where my mother's uncle lived with his wife and two sons on the upper floor.

My mother's uncle, Daei Zamani, was a high-ranking official in the Ministry of Education who came very close to becoming the Minister of Education but did not quite make it. His progressive and liberated wife was among the first women in the country to get her driver's license. She played tennis and poker with men and felt at ease holding her own in the male-dominated Iranian culture.

Our new home had large cheerful rooms, an abundance of sunshine, and French windows overlooking a flowering garden in a good-sized yard. The spacious kitchen with its separate small yard away from the main living quarters was always full of activity.

The new neighborhood was populated by diplomats, doctors, military brass, and high government officials. Overall, it was a wonderful and refreshing change from the dusty alleys of the old neighborhood.

Tehran, a city of nearly three million inhabitants, sat at 5,000 feet above sea level with a panoramic view of the snow-capped Alborz Mountains. The mountain range, although relatively narrow, stretches across northern Iran from Armenia south to the Caspian

Sea and boasts Mt. Damavand, a 19,000 foot, snow-covered volcano and the tallest single mountain in the Middle East.

The pristine atmosphere of fresh mountain air, mixed with an abundance of bright sunshine, gave the earth and its products that unique quality of color which is elusive to describe but readily detectable and admired by painters and photographers. From where we lived, I could easily see the crystal-clear streams and the glittering, tumbling waterfalls tucked between patches of vegetation among the sea of golden-ocher in the surrounding hills.

Tehran represented a proverbial tale of two cities. The northern part, my new home, found itself transforming rapidly into a cosmopolitan town with an insatiable thirst for Western ideas and Western products. Pahlavi street, canopied by ancient sycamores planted along its clear streams, was full of small cafes, restaurants, and boutiques. It connected north of the city to the lap of the Alborz Mountains dotted with villages like Vanak, Shemiran, and Niavaran.

In this part of town, modern homes with European architectural flavors stood side by side with the older traditional homes whose orchards and flower gardens were surrounded by mud and straw walls. In the streets the late-model cars mingled with loaded donkeys and camels.

Here, Islam had little influence. One rarely saw a mullah, and the few mosques here and there kept a low profile.

In contrast, the southern part of Tehran showed little change. Gangs of stray mongrel dogs still wandered among heaps of garbage in the narrow alleys, which were flanked by dilapidated mud and brick houses. Dirty water trickled through crumbling aqueducts, and garbage blanketed the streets and alleys like a polluted lawn.

While the lights of progress shone with full intensity on the northern part of the city, they barely touched the more remote parts of the country. In this agrarian nation, farmers used the same primitive tools as their ancestors had for centuries. Very few roads were paved. The common modes of transport included camels and donkeys. Characteristic of most third-world countries, Iran lacked a substantial middle class and was a country of extremes. The early fifties not only witnessed rapid social and economic changes for the country but also for me.

Two factors played a major role in shifting me from an aimless course to a disciplined purposeful life.

First, was my physical change that transformed me from a short teenager with no self-confidence to a tall, strong young man with a healthy ego and a lot of external positive reinforcement. I discovered girls around this time and, to my great delight, they discovered me back. Second, and equally important, was the nurturing environment of my new school where I began my senior year.

Alborz College had been founded by an American missionary, Dr. Samuel Jordan, as the only boarding school for boys in the country, enrolling students from sixth to twelfth grade. The school's sprawling buildings stretched along the lower hills of the Alborz range where, from the classrooms, the glistening snow-capped summit looked close enough to touch.

In my new environment, I excelled in sports, academics, and mischief. My new self-assurance, combined with optimism and unbridled energy, led me to face the world without fear, confident that my needs would be met and that all my dreams would be fulfilled.

A student whose name, Arastoozadeh, translated as "Descendant of Aristotle," sat in front of me in the classroom. He wore a suit and a fedora, which he placed under his seat. He parted his hair in the middle. His wide, vacant, and expressionless eyes, always red with conjunctivitis, were topped with eyebrows arched in a state of perpetual surprise. I could barely suppress the impulse to crush his hat and pass it on to our fellow classmates. Arastoozadeh's fedora remained a subject of daily conversation in the classroom. But when we became friends and he invited me to his brother's wedding, I realized that the hat was part of his traditional Jewish dress. I felt

THEY CALL ME FERO   53

guilty and embarrassed about nearly turning a potential friend into an enemy before I'd even gotten to know him.

My school attracted students from a variety of religions. There were Muslims, Christians, Zoroastrians, Bahai, Jews, Hindus, atheists, and even casual non-believers like me, who were considered Muslim only by default. We managed to study side by side in total harmony. There was no intolerance or even awareness of a religious otherness.

Friendships formed quickly since most students were new. Among the new circle of friends, I met Nas, a boy from Kerman, a city about 1,000 kilometers south of Tehran at the edge of the central desert that occupies the heart of the country. His family had an unusual and intriguing background.

I never quite learned what his father did, nor do I think Nas himself had a clear understanding of it either.

From the stories I heard, Nas's father was a mover and shaker in local politics. Nas spoke of his father's connections with the British consul as well as his ties with leading local clergy. He spoke of him as being instrumental in bringing people into the streets in support of this or that political cause, setting up for instance an educational center during World War Two in the Kerman district to promote public relations for the British.

I saw photographs of his father in religious attire with a black turban, indicating him as a direct descendant of the prophet Mohamed. In other pictures I saw him sporting modern western clothes.

Though to be a Saied by sharing the same revered genetic pool with the prophet Mohamed carried a lot of weight in the clerical circles, it required no DNA nor any other physical evidence, which opened the door to any would-be descendant who desired to stake a claim. Any opportunist could declare himself as such by simply electing the black turban over the white.

I have no proof one way or the other of Nas's father's claim, nor do I think it an important issue, but I have little difficulty believing that he, like many others, was capable of making such a false declaration.

The father remained an enigma to his own family. Even at the time of his death there was a mystery about his real age. Nas cited it as ninety-six on one occasion and well over a hundred on another. But one had to know Nas a little in order to understand such a discrepancy. Exaggeration and hyperbole were intrinsic to his character.

We called him Nas. But his real name was Saide Malak Nasser Edin. And this was only his first name! The length of his name was a source of light-hearted jokes among our classmates. Though the name Nasser, albeit Arabic in origin, was not an uncommon first name in Iran, it was all the other self promotional trimmings, such as the claims to be a descendent of the prophet Mohamed ("Saide"), and to be connected with royalty ("Malak"), or the connotation of moral superiority ("Edine"), that made it amusing. It was not too hard to see the demagoguery of his father at work in saddling the poor boy with such a cumbersome name, one that Nas himself professed on numerous occasions to despise.

When Nas's father became a widower with four children, he married a recently widowed younger woman with four children of her own. The union of this couple with its houseful of eight children resulted in two more boys. The youngest was Nas.

The family lived together in a large but crowded traditional home in Kerman. One could well imagine the complexity of interactions among such a large and diverse family living so closely under one roof. To add to the chaos, a sister and brother from the father's side married a brother and sister from the mother's side.

The thick atmosphere of rivalry among the siblings in the crowded home nurtured among the siblings certain survival traits second to none. Showmanship and one-upmanship were common characteristics among the siblings. The oldest brother moved to Tehran in search of better opportunities and made a fortune through his construction company. The rest of the family followed him to

Tehran where all nine siblings, through shrewdness, adaptability, and hard work succeeded in their endeavors.

I got to know Nas's colorful family well. They received me warmly, and my mother reciprocated the same way as Nas and I spent countless hours together in each other's houses.

I found Nas interesting for his drive, high creative energy, and shrewd pragmatism. He was intelligent, ambitious, and seemed to have chosen a different path from the rest of his siblings who did not have much education or intellectual interest. Though in many respects we were different, our shared aspirations and common goal of escaping the corrupt and degenerate Iranian society solidified our friendship.

Nas was thin, almost emaciated, and was darker than most of us. He spoke with a noticeable southern accent and was somewhat insecure, finding the new town and its new, cosmopolitan environment perhaps a bit overwhelming. I on the other hand, was sure-footed, adventurous, and confident. I made friends easily.

Nas bought a Lambretta scooter which we often used in high school and in our early days of medical school for transportation. We hiked a lot together, and one day I saw two furry animals on the ridge of hills across from us as we were stretching out after lunch. I pointed them out to Nas and asked what he thought they were.

He said, "Oh. Just stray dogs."

After a moment, I said, "Are you sure? Look again."

Nas looked, and we said at the same time, "Wolves!"

I don't think either of us had ever run so fast down a mountain.

Another time, we took a trip around the Caspian Sea in an old Chevrolet that he had borrowed from his brother. The car was so rusty we could see the ground through the holes in the floor. By some miracle we managed to coax the car over the winding mountain roads but lost one of the back wheels as we were driving on the level ground along the sea. We slept on the side of the road overnight, and the following day, we flagged down a charcoal-carrying lorry and caught a ride to the next town. By the time we reached our destination, we were completely blackened. It took us a few days to have the car fixed and nearly as long to scrub the charcoal soot from our faces and bodies.

Nas's family received me as one of their own and mine reciprocated. As frequent guest in our family, he attended the weekend parties we often had during the years we shared a house with my mother's uncle. Those years were among the most memorable of my life in Iran.

The big kitchen away from the main building was always busy with women preparing food for guests. We had parties during weekends and danced to European and Latin American music in the upstairs salon where family and friends gathered. There was talk, laughter, and the background music of Ella Fitzgerald, Nat King Cole, Frank Sinatra, and Dean Martin.

In our large family, there were many weddings to which everybody was invited. Weddings were held mostly in clubs or hotels with a liberal flow of alcohol and much dancing with an orchestra that played both Persian and Western music.

It was customary for brides and grooms to open the dance floor with the well-known tango, *la Cumpasita*, a popular Uruguayan tune composed in 1917. This particular melody, as I understand it, has been customarily played in Latin America at the end of a ceremony to signify that the party is over. Could it be that the wise men of Persia ironically played this tune at the beginning, knowing that, for the new couple, the party was over now that the wedding had started?

When I wasn't socializing or partying with friends and family, I burned off my excess energy through sports.

At school I played soccer, volleyball, and tennis. But my real love was climbing mountains in the Alborz range.

I remember like yesterday the villages close to the city where the earth was covered with the golden leaves of early autumn.

I was gathered around a campfire with a group of my uncle's friends sipping tea after a long day's hike. The city below had surrendered to darkness. Occasional flickers of street lights here and there gave the only indication that life in the darkened city below still existed. The evening was gently cool with a breeze whispering through the bare trees. In the distance, a donkey brayed, and out of the darkness, a dog responded. Someone played harmonica. The melody was the famous Cuban-inspired La Paloma, and everyone hummed along. The moment and the music seared their imprints on me indelibly.

By the time I was seventeen I spent most weekends in the mountains, sometimes with friends, but often alone.

During such weekends I took the public bus very early in the morning to the small village of Darband where the narrow path of the rocky gorge began. A bronze statue of a young man with his climbing gear stood as if in permanent observation of the mountain. I nodded a joyous greeting to him.

I took the path along the river and past glistening boulders. I zigzagged up the steep cobble-stoned path by the peasants' humble cottages with their bright blue shutters and their small yards where roosters, goats, and donkeys mingled with children and where women performed their daily chores. Further up, I passed the tea houses with their wide wooden benches placed by the side of the river for customers to enjoy the view.

Leaving behind the slumbering village and its crowing roosters, I reached the open space where the expansive sky met the glistening snow of the summit. In the invigorating cold air, I traversed the flank of the gentle hill while the rays of the early morning sun transformed the mountain range into a sea of gold, revealing the vegetation around the rivulets and waterfalls halfway up.

Happy and content, I had all I needed. My packed sandwiches, fruits and nuts and warm clothing in my back pack, pure melting water of the mountain, and a world full of promises that affirmed eventual freedom and independence from the tedium of daily life.

I kept climbing, anticipating the tough crossing of the rocky section that would lead to the secluded, pristine waterfall with its familiar aroma of garden angelica and the host of wild flowers growing in the higher altitudes. Their solitary fragrance stirred a unique surge of happiness in me. I knew every step, every rock, every tree, and every fragrance along the way.

Mountains drew me like a magnet. Climbing has been an important element in my sense of spirituality and in shaping me into the man I've become. I felt rejuvenated, empowered as if stepping out of myself and able to see the world with an outsider's view. I gazed into a new horizon beyond the ordinary and away from the minutia of everyday life. I felt close to the source of life and experienced a powerful kinship with the elements around me. After all, wasn't God supposed to be in the sky, the same sky I could now very nearly reach out and touch?

Perspiring and pleasantly fatigued, I reached the twin waterfalls. I bathed under the cold heavy pressure of the waterfall and took a nap beneath the pleasant warmth of the sun. Lulled by the murmuring of the currents, I had some of the most wonderful dreams.

Returning in the twilight, the city with its flickering lights looked serene and quiet. I felt like an outsider looking in, an observer with a greater power over the city than those who had never left it.

For a while I became interested in technical rock climbing. The sport was then in its infancy in Iran, and our tools and equipment were primitive. When a friend lost his grip on a climb and broke his back, the incident put an end to my interest in hard-core rock climbing, but my love for mountains, especially high-altitude hiking, continued. I introduced the sport to some friends, but other than Nas, few others accompanied me.

Once I organized an ambitious ten-day trek across the mountains and the valleys where Hassan Sabbah, the notorious leader of a group of assassins had terrorized the country for decades during the fourteenth century. He had run his underground organization from the castles at the remote peaks of this region called the Summit of Alamoot. In order to make it more of an adventure, I insisted no one bring money or extra provisions beyond the most basic necessities of our excursion. There were seven of us, among them Nas, Homayoon, and Houshang. We started from the southern lap of the Alborz range where Tehran is situated and planned to go over a few passes and finish on the other side through the lush vegetation and forests along the Caspian Sea where we had arranged for Homayoon's family car and driver to meet us at a designated point.

The plan went more or less according to schedule but the last thirty-six hours or so we were left with only a small amount of rice and very little money. We reached the bank of a shallow river close to our rendezvous for the following day and settled down for the night. A few of us were suffering from upset stomachs, and everyone felt quite hungry. We decided to stop at the nearest village and spend our last few coins on yogurt, which is known for its nutritional value and its beneficial effect in combatting diarrhea. We opened the bottle of vodka we had saved for the last evening to celebrate our successful adventure and toasted repeatedly. The evening was overcast, and darkness was enveloping us fast. While the others continued toasting and drinking, I started to cook the rice. In the final stages of the cooking, the pot tipped over and spilled our dinner onto the sandy bank of the river. The hungry group, unaware of my clumsy accident, anxiously waited and kept asking when the rice was coming. I could hear Hooshang's and Homayoon's distinct voices above the others and the banging of their utensils against their empty plates. I had no choice but to scoop up as carefully as I could the mixture of rice and sand. The inedible food ruined my reputation as a cook forever. And with the so-called dinner fixed in their memories, they never let me set foot in the kitchen at our subsequent social gatherings.

MY PARENTS

ROCK CLIMBING IN ALBORZ MOUNTAIN

TOUCHAL SUMMIT, ALBORZ MOUNTAIN. AMIR (LEFT) WITH ME ON THE RIGHT

WITH MOTHER AND MY SISTER MARIAM

6. IRAN AND THE GREAT GAME

My senior year at Alborz College in 1953 and the subsequent six years at the medical school coincided with one of the most politically turbulent eras for the country. During this period, Alborz College and Tehran University were two of the hotbeds of political activism. Together, they played a central role in leading the rest of the nation.

Iran, no stranger to international political struggle, had been at the center of cross-currents representing the colonial interests in the Middle East and central Asia, a political epoch dubbed by political historians as "the Great Game." The dominant players were Great Britain and Russia, followed by the U.S., France, and Germany.

The British wanted to secure a stable region surrounding their colonial interests in India and to protect their huge oil reserves in the region under control of British Petroleum.

The Russians' brazen expansionist policy of reaching the strategically important waters of the Persian Gulf had been openly declared from the time of Peter the Great. This goal had been persistently pursued throughout Russia's tumultuous political past. Historically most of the present provinces that form the southern flank of Russia, were annexed from Iran as recently as the mid-19th century.

Though Iran was never formally colonized or ruled by foreign nations, the country was never free from the intrusive policies of foreign powers, especially Great Britain and Russia. Their brutal and imperialistic designs left the country in a deplorable state.

To break the stranglehold of Britain and Russia, who by this time had full control of the financial affairs of the country, Majlis (Irans' parliament) voted in 1911 to appoint an American financier named Morgan Schuster to remedy the sorry state of Iran's financial affairs. This did not sit well with the Russians. Their tanks rolled through the streets of Tehran and their troops shut down the Iranian parliament. Then in 1925, against the desire of the British, who had a monopoly over the oil reserves of Iran, Reza Shah (the Shah's father) granted concessions of an oil exploration to the Standard Oil Company of New Jersey. Franklin D. Roosevelt believed that America could provide badly needed help to remedy the appalling misery that the competing exploitation by Russia and England had created in Iran. This was the beginning of the involvement of the United States as the new player among the old hands in the Great Game.

The most important individual during political crisis in the years of 1914-1953 was an Iranian nationalist and political figure named Dr. Mossadegh.

Mossadegh was born into an old aristocratic family and was a descendant of the previous ruling dynasty which Reza Shah had replaced. He was exposed from an early age to the intrigues of the ruling class, groomed to be a political leader. He left Iran to study law in France and returned when Reza Shah was in power. He became active in politics and pursued the always dying but never quite dead idea of constitutional rights. He wanted more power for the people and less for the heavy-handed monarch, Reza Shah. He fought against the Capitulation Treaties, under which foreigners were given special legal rights protecting them from being tried under the Iranian judicial system. The treaty that made Iranians second-rate citizens in their own country.

Mossadegh's political views and opposition to Reza Shah placed him under house arrest for many years. During this time he tried to improve the standard of life of more than 150 families working for him in a self-sufficient community called Ahmadabad on the outskirts of the capital. During this period, he focused on his second love, medicine, and organized a well-stocked dispensary of herbal remedies. He personally ran the facility until his son, who also became a physician, took over.

According to Motahedeh, a history professor at Princeton, "Guests who visited him during this period of time, had to have the courage to swallow the spoonful of a bitter extract of boiled juniper berries," which he offered to all, believing it would "clear the system and be beneficial for many afflictions."

The political landscape began to change when Allied forces invaded Iran in the summer of 1941. The invasion was to assure a safe corridor in order to transport supplies to the Russian front against the Germans. Reza Shah's token resistance against the Allies and his overt flirtation with Germany, forced his abdication, and his young son was installed as the new monarch.

With Reza Shah in exile, the time was right for Dr. Mossadegh to come out of house arrest. Shortly after his release, he was elected with the overwhelming support of the people of the Tehran district as their representative to parliament. As a Member of Parliament, fully supported by the nation, he nationalized the Iranian Oil Company and banned any future discussion of oil concessions with foreigners.

The British Petroleum Oil Cowpony, having a complete monopoly over the vast oil industry of Iran, reimbursed the country next to nothing. Their condescending and arrogant attitude toward

Iranians, treating them as an inferior class, deeply wounded Iranian national pride.

In 1953, my senior year at Alborz College, I witnessed a significant political awakening for Iran and a heightened awareness among intellectuals. The two centers of political unrest, Alborz College and Tehran University were highly charged with various ideologies, and no one remained neutral. The most popular organization was the national political movement led by then Prime Minister Dr. Mossadegh. He was considered a lightning rod of national political awareness and had enormous support throughout the nation.

The two years he served as the prime minister of Iran, during which he campaigned against the exploitation of the oil companies and the imperialistic international policy of foreign powers, are as much part of the world's history as the Iranian nation itself. He was easily the most visible and globally recognized leader during this period. Nationalization of Iran's oil industry was a great blow to the British economy.

A masterful actor, Dr. Mossadegh could bring out the whole nation in the streets to demonstrate in support of his cause. He was the first Iranian leader who utilized radio and newspapers with maximum efficiency to reach the people and his goals. The Iranian nationalist movement became a role model for other nations in the region, and Dr. Mossadegh, admired for his opposition to colonial intervention and for his promotion of internal democratic reforms, was named *Time Magazine's* "Man of the Year" in 1951.

Jamal-Abdul-Nasser followed the same anti-imperialist path in Egypt, creating another major headache around 1956 for the British and French by nationalizing the Suez Canal, an act which ultimately led to the Suez Canal crisis.

Mossadegh was an eccentric man with habits evoking curiosity among Iranians and the outside world. He conducted the most important business of the country in bed and in his pajamas under gray, woolen blankets. He wept publicly when deeply moved. He appeared weak and had frequent fainting spells, yet according to Mottahedh, in his book titled *The Mantle of the Prophet*, "He was strong enough to rip the arm off a chair in the chamber of Parliament when, in a passion of speech, he wanted something to wave in the air at an opponent." For the western world, he was hard to figure out. The British were devastated by his policies, and the Americans were confused by his eccentricity.

Nevertheless, the overt and covert activities of the foreign powers in the region continued, and the new actors took the place of the old. While the influence of the British diminished, the Russian influence increased in Iran through the strengthening of the Communist Party, particularly among intellectuals and students. Flirtation of the nationalist movement led by Mossadegh with the Communist Party, who also shared the same goal of opposing the regime under the Shah, raised eyebrows in Washington. This was during the Cold War, an era with an exaggerated global paranoia about the spread of Communism. Using the same logic that had been rejected by Harry Truman's administration repeatedly, the CIA finally convinced the new Eisenhower administration to undermine the Iranian National movement and to support the Shah.

A plot, code named "Operation Ajax," was formulated by the CIA in collaboration with British Intelligence. The covert operation changed the destiny of Iran and with it initiated a chain reaction of events throughout the Middle East, the repercussions of which continue to resonate in the region to this day.

In 1953, the Shah made an unsuccessful attempt to replace Mossadegh as the prime minister. Mossadegh refused to step down, claiming his legitimacy by the overwhelming support of the people. When the military also refused to remove him, the Shah, under the pretense of taking a vacation, left the country for Italy.

Through a rent-a-crowd demonstration, led by a local bully nicknamed Shaban bee Mokh, or "Shaban the Brainless," and in collaboration with the few military officers under general Zahedi, individuals were recruited for a dollar a day to engage in mob activity. Demanding the return of the Shah and claiming to represent the will of the people, they got Mossadegh placed under house arrest. The red carpet was rolled out for the Shah's return, placing him back on the peacock throne.

The total cost of "Operation Ajax" was estimated at around $100,000. The plan worked. The Shah came to power, and Dr. Mossadegh was deposed along with the progressive and nationalist reforms he had undertaken.

American names mentioned in association with Operation Ajax were Kermit Roosevelt, a resourceful CIA agent who played a central role in coordinating the plot with the British Intelligence in Iran; General Schwarzkopf (father of the commander of Desert Storm); John Foster Dulles, the Secretary of State; and his brother Allen Dulles, Director of the CIA.

On the Iranian side among the key players were Ashraf, twin sister of the Shah; general Zahedi; Ayatollah Kashani; and General Zahedi's son, Ardeshir, who married the Shah's daughter shortly after and became Iranian ambassador to Washington where he was well known for lavish parties and generous gift-giving.

The long-term effect of the coup is seen by many historians as a significant factor in fomenting many political upheavals in the region. Many historians point to this U.S.-inspired-coup as the catalyst for decades of regional political unrest.

Stephen Kinzer a foreign correspondent for the New York Times in his book *All the Shah's Men* writes:

It is a reasonable argument that but for the coup, Iran would be a mature democracy. So traumatic was the coup's legacy that when the Shah finally departed in 1979, many Iranians feared the repetition of 1953, which was one of the motivations for the student seizure of the US embassy. The hostage crisis, in turn, precipitated the Iraq invasion of Iran, while the (Islamic) revolution itself played a part in the Soviet decision to invade Afghanistan. A lot of history, in short, flowed from a single week in Tehran. The 1953 coup and its consequences were the starting point for the political alignments in today's Middle East and inner Asia. With hindsight, can anybody say that the Islamic Revolution of 1979 was inevitable? Or did it only become so once the aspirations of the Iranian people were temporarily expunged in 1953?

Kinzer asks, "How did Iran reach the tragic crossroads of August 1953?" And responds by putting the blame squarely on the greedy British Petroleum company and just as much on the British government.

Dean Acheson had it exactly right, Kinzer says, when he wrote, "Never had so few lost so much so stupidly and so fast."

Though the behind-the-scenes activities of the American and British governments were known to many Iranians, surprisingly it took forty-seven years for the U.S. administration to declassify the CIA Iranian plot of 1953. Americans remained unaware for nearly five decades about the role their country played in Iran's destiny.

During these politically turbulent years, Alborz College and Tehran University where I continued my education were a hotbed of demonstrations and daily clashes with police. Most of us supported the national movement. Mossadegh was a leader who for the first time in our young lives had stood for the principles over politics. Few students escaped interrogation by the police. Many students were detained or were forced to spend time in the dreaded Evin Prison.

The military stationed in Alborz College arrested nearly any group consisting of more than four or five students. When I found myself in the middle of classmates surrounded by a circle of soldiers, I managed to get away, but those who did not were detained. During the roll call in our next class when the names of the missing were called, "Evin Prison" was uttered by some. They all had stories to tell, and some students paid the ultimate price with their lives. I knew personally two of the victims who were killed during such demonstrations in Tehran University.

The schizophrenic history of Persian culture is replete with a cyclical duality of the prevailing power between secular and religious sentiments.

My mother's generation was brought up under a strict Islamic rule of law that governed the country, while I watched it change one hundred and eighty degrees when Reza Shah's secular regime dealt with Islamic rules violently, aggressively attacking religious institutions. During this period, any man with a turban would be at risk. Any woman who dared to go out with a veil would be subject to its forced removal. Reza Shah's government had a zero-tolerance policy for religious rituals. Muslims were marginalized, and Reza Shah closed many religious schools and centers for training the clergy.

In past almost thirty years, since the Islamic Revolution, the pendulum has swung back, and we have seen the resurgence of the religious fundamentalism in Iran, this time with an equally harsh zero-tolerance policy toward secularism.

This identity crisis, which is deeply rooted in the psyche of the Iranian culture, stems from the schism that has always been present among Iranians from the early days of the Arab invasion when, as the conquerors of the Persian Empire, leaders imposed Islam as the official religion of the country.

During the time I grew up in the country, most Iranians saw themselves as Aryans whose forebears inhabited the Iranian plateau more than 5,000 years ago with their own religion of Zoroastrianism. They believed that within evolutionary consciousness of civilized man, Zoroastrianism had been among the main contributors in forming the foundation of other major religions of the world such as Judaism and Christianity. They held that Persian culture, which dominated the ancient world for a considerable period, had been a major contributor along with Greek and Roman cultures in creating the underpinnings of our global civilization as we know it today.

When Islam conquered the Persian Empire, it was the influence of Persian culture that rejuvenated and provided the cultural sustenance needed to maintain the forward momentum. Arabs were a collection of primitive tribes still leading nomadic lives in the vast deserts of the Arabian Peninsula. This was the common sentiment highly touted by the secular regime as I was growing up in Iran.

Pt. II – Becoming a Doctor

7. MEDICAL SCHOOL CALLS MY NAME

Meaningful social change started in Iran when the well-intentioned and heavy-handed dictator Reza Shah began a major reform by building the foundation for a modern society. Reza Shah was an illiterate but courageous soldier who ascended the military ranks to the top and, through a successful coup d'etat, created the new Pahlavi Dynasty in 1921.

Prior to the secular regime of Reza Shah, Iran's illiteracy rate was among the highest in the world. Access to schooling beyond sixth grade was limited to a handful of schools in the big cities, and higher education was non-existent except for those select few who could afford to travel abroad.

Reza Shah's administration laid the foundation for the educational system of the country. Shortly after he was crowned in 1921, the capital's first institute of higher learning, Tehran University, was founded.

By the time I left the country as a 25-year-old medical school graduate in 1960, Iran had become a much different country from the Persia I remembered during my younger years.

Tehran Medical School had become a highly prized centerpiece of the new university system. The school's faculty was a mix of the best and brightest graduates of European and American universities, and the school's facilities, including its laboratories and the teaching hospitals, were on a par with better schools in the West. Although by then, two or three other medical schools were founded in other provinces, Tehran Medical School remained the preeminent institution of its kind in Iran and was sought-after by high school graduates throughout the country.

The year I took the entrance examination for admission into the freshman class, few thousands of high school graduates as usual applied for two hundred and fifty spots.

Unhappy with the limited opportunities available in Iran and deeply disillusioned with the governmental corruption, I wanted to leave the country. I was willing to consider any opportunity providing such possibilities, convinced I had a better chance to realize my potential in the western world.

I considered law, but my father rejected the idea and discouraged me at every turn. The Navy and Air Force appealed to me, the former for its romantic and remote ports of call, and the latter for the opportunity to fly.

In the end, I registered and was accepted in the Naval Academy with the understanding that I would be going to England for my training.

But the challenge of the demanding entrance exam to the medical school was too tempting to resist. As confident as I was though, I could not be certain of the outcome. I was not dedicated enough to study with the intensity that seemed the prerequisite for getting through the entrance exam of Tehran Medical School. I had no pressing desire to join the other prospective medical school students in their obsessive studying and endless fretting over the entrance exam. Most participants had already taken the exam several times and were desperate to pass.

Unable to back away from the challenge, I decided to give it a try. The night before the exam, unlike most students who remained glued to their books, I went to see the performance of an outdoor play. It was far too nice a night, I reasoned, to waste it on the stress of studying.

A few weeks after the exam, quite early in the morning, the telephone rang. A classmate had heard my name on the radio among those accepted for the medical school. He had called to congratulate me.

Incredulous, I asked, "Are you sure it was my name?"

"Yes," he said. "I'm sure."

My heart raced. I was excited and proud to see the joy on the faces of my father and mother and sister who, having heard my conversation, had gathered around the phone. After they congratulated me, I left to see for myself the list posted on the main entrance of the university. After a tediously long bus ride, I arrived at the university where a crowd of students had gathered in front of the iron gates. I joined the noisy crowd, jostling for position, leaning in and trying to read from the typed list of names. I caught my name on the third sheet well within the top third of the candidates. How wonderfully different my name seemed on its typed-written form, standing out, glowing with hope, vibrant with potential and promise. When I got back home and confirmed for my family my high place in the list of candidates, they cheered me on and called me "Doctor"! The word sounded so delicious, so foreign, and so right.

Acceptance to the medical school created a life of its own. The fanfare and the excitement of friends and family, announcements of the names of the freshman class in all the papers and the radio, and the personal euphoria of success in such a tough competition created a momentum forceful enough to catapult me through the crowded doors of the university into the freshman class of Tehran Medical School where I would study for the next six years.

I was eighteen-years-old at the time, a teenager giddily charmed by the world. I welcomed its challenges and saw no reason to believe that the future would be any less pleasing than the sum of my experiences. I was quite certain my future would be rewarding regardless of the path I took. Therefore when I faced the two radically different futures, navy or medicine, I did not hesitate to choose. It was many years later that I learned of Yogi Bera's motto: "When you come to a fork in the road, take it." And so I did.

I said goodbye to the open seas and to the imagined visits to ports of call and began to prepare myself for six years of a demanding and studious life.

I am awed by the powerful and ever-present duality deep in our psyche, which influences the way we perceive our universe. Why are some blessed with the capacity to overlook and ignore negative aspects of life, able to focus on a spots that shine in the midst of rubbish, while others could dwell only on the darker side, unable to see the beauty of the world? Is it surprising then that men could look at an identical situation and see two totally different things?

Kierkegaard describes the negative element of this duality:

If you get married, you regret it; if you do not get married, you regret it. If you have children, you regret it; if you do not have children you regret it. If you divorce your wife, you regret it; if you do not divorce your wife, you regret it. If you hang yourself you regret it; if you do not hang yourself you will regret that too.

My psychology tends toward identifying blessings over dwelling on regrets. This sanguine prism through which I have perceived the world has been a marvelous means of helping me through my travels and life experiences. I am amazed at how often people fret and stress over choices in their lives. Each choice has consequences, of course, but we must not let that distract us from realizing and appreciating the truth: Having choices at all is the real blessing.

How, I wonder, could we not be grateful for the opportunity to witness the magic our world has to offer?

Statistically we are chosen out of billions of other germinating cells, each with an equal hidden potential to have replaced us.

We have overcome millions of obstacles during the course of a few months of gestation and during the short journey from the cervix to the womb.

We are living in an era of human civilization that has required billions of evolutionary years to achieve the present maturity of cosmic consciousness where we find ourselves among our fellow men.

Whether by design, chance, or a selective process, how could we not be awed by our presence in this world? How could we not appreciate and enjoy the moment? And yet most do not. "Life is a banquet," Oscar Wilde said, "but most S.O.B.'s, are starving."

For a long while, I chalked up my entry into the medical field as pure chance. Years later, deeply immersed in my medical practice with so much satisfaction, I began to suspect that certain specific experiences had played a role in nudging me toward my chosen field.

As a child and then as a teenager, I had been guided by events, which I had dismissed at the time as irrelevant abstractions, just more of life's busyness to be endured and forgotten. But so much of it has stayed with me. Standing on the imposing university doorstep, ready to embark on a demanding adventure, I thought back to the soothing visits of our family physician Dr. Ganjbaksh. When my body battled against a deadly strain of Typhus, Dr. Ganjbaksh stood by my side. Armed with little more than herbal medicine and an assuring presence, he fought the disease with me. Aided perhaps by my grandmother's prayers, Dr. Ganjbaksh was triumphant in boosting my young immune system to complete what my family to this day calls a "miraculous recovery."

Of course, I also remember the callousness of Dr. Radji who refused to treat our maid when she fell and broke her arm. "I no longer take care of maids," he said, and I found myself disappointed and disgusted at his arrogance. His exclusive focus on helping only the upper class struck me, even at my young age, as the height of narcissism and as an affront to the universality of the human spirit.

So two doctors from two different ends of the humanitarian spectrum had unknowingly but thankfully helped guide me into a career that would offer personal fulfillment, but more importantly, that would allow me to provide personal fulfillment to others in their times of physical and emotional distress.

8. A DELICIOUSLY TEMPTING WORLD

As my professional career and ambitions got under way, my social life followed suit. Things were coming together for me academically so why not romantically as well?

After a year or two of hesitant flirting, my first real romantic encounter was with a sixteen-year-old distant relative who lived in a compound of houses a few blocks away from us.

The patriarch of this family was Arbab Gholam Husien, a bachelor landowner in his sixties. He was a short man with a big head and deep gray eyes. He hung around the house all day except when attending to some of his properties in his long, chauffeur driven blue Chrysler. He had made considerable money through real estate and had taken five of his orphan nieces and two of his orphan nephews under his wing. The whole bunch lived with him in the big house or in adjoining houses in the compound.

With typical Persian over-attention to boys, he wound up spoiling the two nephews, turning them as adults into alcoholics who drank lots and accomplished little.

Kazem the older of the two nephews, had a beautiful daughter named Parnaz.

At her sixteenth birthday party, Parnaz and I danced all night to the music of a small band playing in the reception room of the big house. Parnaz wore a blue velvet dress and looked radiant. She had jet black hair, starry black eyes, and dark close-set eyebrows, all the hallmarks of the classic Persian beauties. We danced over and over to "Besame Mucho" and "Blue Tango." To this day, those songs remind me of Parnaz in her blue velvet dress.

Parnaz and I met afterward at family gatherings and at weekend parties now and then. I knew our families viewed us as a great match. The idea was not far fetched after all, since two of her aunts had married two of my uncles. I could see the Iranian pastime of matchmaking hard at work.

The month of Ramadan and its routine religious gathering of "Rozeh Khani" in the big house provided the opportunity for us to meet. Parnaz wrapped in a chador, met me secretly in a secluded room. Slipping the veil away, we stole away together. I held her tight in my arms, anxiously listening for approaching footsteps. We kissed for the first time as she whispered, "Fraydoon, dooset daram," I love you.

And there were other times that we met in the garden:

The warmth of the summer day is rapidly diminishing by the cool evening breeze, redolent with the scent of blooming jasmine. I light a cigarette and wait for Parnaz behind the bushes. She appears a moment later wearing a polka-dot cotton dress with a flared skirt topped with a thin, pink mohair blouse buttoned up to where her teasingly-low collar ends. Her narrow waist accentuates her shapely breasts. I hold her close, pressing my face against her Nina Ricci perfumed hair as she whispers repeatedly, "Dooset daram." I meet her warm eager lips and watch her soft yielding eyes, still discernible in the enveloping darkness.

I was a freshman in medical school on the path to discovering a deliciously tempting world, anticipating my graduation from medical school in five years, and going abroad for my specialty.

Marriage was not on the radar screen for my foreseeable future. I conveyed the message loud and clear.

Parnaz understood and eventually gave in to the relentless matchmaking pressure of the family and married a man with a meager education who was assumed to have lots of money but as it turned out owed more than he owned. Years later she divorced him and settled in the U.S. where she became a successful designer of women's clothing.

Socially, the more progressive Iranians had just begun to accept the intermingling of men and women as a prudent step before committing to marriage, but the majority still followed the traditions of the arranged marriage. I was around ten when my father told my mother that one of his colleagues from the Ministry of Justice, Mr. Hameedi had recently been transferred from Hamedan and was looking for a wife. My father thought that the colleague was a good candidate for his niece. Ghodrat my father's niece, was a shy, average-looking twenty-year-old who perhaps was considered something of an old maid already according to Iranian culture. It didn't help her cause that if nervous, she had a tendency to be cross-eyed.

My father invited the colleague for lunch in order to introduce him to Ghodrat.

Mr. Hameedi was soft spoken and shy, always demure and quick to blush. At one point during the dinner, Mr. Hameedi, after a few minutes of discreet observation, asked my father in French if Ghodrat was indeed cross-eyed. My father with his usual tact denied it loudly in Farsi and demanded Ghodrat to look up at him. Holding her by her chin, he turned to Mr. Hameedi and asked him still in Farsi, "Do those eyes look crossed to you?" It was an awkward moment to say the least. I felt especially bad for the poor young woman who blushed deeply. But at the same time, I was happy for her sake to see that, whether by sheer determination or pure luck, her eyes at that moment anyway, were as straight as arrows.

Most arranged marriages involved a lot of haggling, bargaining, maneuvering, and negotiating before the final agreement, much of it without input from the two essential parties: The bride and the groom.

To bring the story to its happy ending, Ghodrat and Mr. Hameedi married. He became a well-known judge. Their long marriage, by all accounts, was harmonious and prosperous. Decades later, on one of my visits to Iran, I spoke with Ghodrat. I learned that Mr. Hameedi had died a few years earlier. She missed him terribly. She had aged well, and was cheerful and proud of her successful children.

True, for a majority of the young generation especially the women, dating was not an option and remained taboo, but for some, the opportunities were abundantly available.

Most young men married early. Those who did not, visited the red light district known as *Shahre-no* with brothels clustered in a few blocks within the city. I avoided those places. I needed real relationships and found one not too far from where I lived.

It was a few blocks away from ours, where adult education classes for English language were conducted by an English woman during the evenings, that I saw Simin for the first time.

Simin was an elegantly dressed, very attractive brunette in her thirties with lusty brown eyes that held mine long enough to leave their mark behind.

A few nights later, I walked past her class with the hope of seeing her again. Our eyes searched each other out, this time with eagerness and warmth.

Inquiring about her, I learned she was recently divorced from an influential government official and had lived in France.

A few months later at a Christmas party at the English woman's home, I saw her with some of her classmates, but she never took her eyes off me. I was full of narcissistic self-discovery mixed with a heavy dose of awareness of my popularity with the opposite sex, all of which stroked my ego.

I walked daily to school through the side streets where she lived and where I knew I would find her waiting for me at her doorstep or in her red and white Opel.

After months of obsessing over her, I finally decided to call her.

"You don't know me," I said, "but I see you often."

"Yes," she replied, "and I wait for you often. You were a little late this afternoon."

"What is your name?" I asked.

"Simin."

"My name is Fraydoon."

"I know," she replied.

That was the beginning of many phone conversations, after which I found her more frequently at her door. I still did not have the courage to stop and talk. What would the neighbors think?

I had a tremendous desire for her and found it quite hard to continue to walk when she asked me to come in for a moment. "Just for a moment."

"Nobody is home," she said. "I am alone."

A few days after that, I returned the favor when I also found myself home alone. She came over, as if stepping out of a fashion magazine. I was worried, not knowing when my parents would return. She did not stay long but the warmth and the softness of her kisses stayed with me long after her departure. Her perfume lingered, and I had to open all the doors and windows before my parents got back.

As a voracious, hot-blooded nineteen-year-old, it was impossible to resist this seductive thirty-year-old beauty. I had a much easier time of rationalizing the moral aspect of such a relationship by convincing myself that the pleasing act of two consenting adult was okay as long as it did not hurt others.

On one late afternoon, returning from school, I stepped into her house and we turned into a room right off the foyer. We kissed hungrily, and her beige satin robe slipped to the floor. Holding her gave me much the same thrill as I'd experienced as a young boy when my anxious lips had traversed the full spectrum of that soft sweetness of the crème cone for the first time. In Simin's radiating eyes, I could see her pleasure and delight of guiding me through the erotic journey.

We enjoyed an intense relationship, which continued on and off for a few years before gradually fading as other women entered my life.

9. MY ODYSSEY THROUGH MEDICAL SCHOOL

When I wasn't thinking about Simin, I was thinking about other women. When I wasn't thinking about them, I focused what little attention I had left on my medical school studies.

Six of us from my class at Alborz College had passed the entrance examination and entered the medical school.

The challenging first three years of medical school dealt with basic sciences.

In the first year, we studied mostly anatomy with an extraordinary emphasis on detail, almost to the point of obsession. Every ramification of branches of an artery or vein, the most obscure and unimportant muscles or tendons, needed to be memorized and identified. Although these exercises seemed futile at the time, their importance became clear to me years later when I became a surgeon.

In school, I spent hours every morning memorizing the anatomy books and in the afternoons, many more hours performing dissections in the cadaver room.

Friendships among our group from Alborz continued, and we saw a lot of each other during this period. There were also new friends including an inseparable pair, Reza and Parviz. Known for their dedication and hard work, they were academically among the top students in the class. Never apart, they sat together in the front row of the class where they took copious notes. They never missed a word. And since not all subjects taught were published or available in print, notes taken during classes were essential.

We did our endless hours of studies in groups of two or three. I joined Reza and Parviz to study, though I was no match for their single-minded determination when it came to review, especially during the summer recess as we prepared for our final exams. During such periods, we met in one of the hot, bare rooms of Reza's house where he lived with his grandmother. We began early in the morning. One read aloud, and the other two listened. Since I skipped many classes and did not have reliable notes, I never read and always listened, or at least tried to. Distracted by the persistent buzzing of flies or by the aroma of frying eggplant coming from the kitchen or focused on the monotonous cooing of the pigeons on the rooftop, my mind wandered during the long hours. By the time the sun began to set, I would lose interest in listening and would switch over to ruminating about dates, parties, and the wonderful world waiting outside.

"I'll catch up later," I always promised Reza and Parviz. Then I'd leave.

The demanding first three years of medical school revolved around basic science courses and allowed little time for anything else. The fourth year and the beginning of our clinical rotations, however, gave us more room to breathe and expanded my social calendar.

To meet the demands of my social activities, I needed money. The government funded all but a nominal fee of my medical school tuition. Since my father covered the expense of my medical books and paraphernalia, and also provided pocket money, I did not think I should ask him for more.

A longtime friend and a classmate from the eighth grade who worked in the Iranian National Oil Company, aware of my need for extra cash, offered to split his monthly salary with me, with the understanding that I would pay him back when I could.

Mansour was quiet and shy. He was a good and loyal friend. We hiked frequently during weekends and climbed the 15,000 foot summit of Tochal, just to the north of Tehran, many times together. For climbing Tochal, we left the city very early and spent the night in a little stone hut built on a plateau two thirds up the mountain. We left the hut in the wee hours of the morning in order to reach the summit in time to see the rising sun.

Mansour left Iran a few years later to continue his education in Germany. Aware of his limited resources and his upcoming expenses in a foreign land, I paid him back well in excess of the amount I had borrowed. Mansour's generosity touched me deeply, since his financial strength was limited and my needs were not especially dire. I lost contact with him since his departure for Germany and made periodic attempts to track him down but without success.

Among other non-medical school friends was a group of architects. Though not yet graduated and still in their final year of architecture school, they already had developed busy practices. This was when Tehran was expanding at an astronomical pace, and architects had no trouble finding work. My architect friends worked in a spacious, light-filled office in a nice section of town. Jokes, laughter, and classical music suffused their workplace. I joined them whenever I could, mostly late in the evening, and we often left together to go to restaurants or night clubs. If I had a special date, I would exchange my VW beetle for their more comfortable and luxurious 1958 Citroen, a car to die for at the time.

It was around the end of my third year at medical school when my father bought me a brand-new silver VW Beetle. Having wheels at this juncture was a great help since it coincided with the clinical rotations which required us to go to different hospitals scattered throughout the city.

Routinely I stayed out late in those years, drove recklessly, and loved to speed. I appeared time and again in front of judges for traffic violations and just as often was let go without any fine, out of respect for my father.

In the Fifties, Tehran still remained among the least congested cities with few cars in the streets. The police had just formed a new branch to control traffic through a small cadre of special officers with shiny new motorcycles and vibrant uniforms.

One of these officer caught me speeding late one evening. He nabbed me again a few nights later for having only one headlight. When he asked to see my license, I had to remind him that he already had taken it just a few nights earlier. We got to know each other pretty well, and he began greeting me by name whenever he pulled over the silver beetle with one headlight.

I was not born with a silver spoon in my mouth. I had seen more than my share of poverty when we lived in the southern part of the city. Nevertheless, I found the depth of poverty and misery during my clinical rotation to be truly appalling.

It was nearly impossible to witness the shivering, barely-clothed patients in the dead of winter and still maintain the necessary clinical distance. On more than one occasion, I gave away an overcoat or whatever warm jacket I might be wearing, and my family often wondered what kept happening to all of my sweaters.

Pahlavi Hospital was the main teaching hospital for the medical school and, like most such hospitals, it took care of indigents. But unlike most teaching hospitals in the U.S., there was little if any supervision. Residents or interns had free reign in treating the patients, sometimes with disastrous results.

The types and varieties of medical conditions we dealt with were different from the garden varieties seen in the West.

Infectious diseases of all sorts took a huge toll and were the dominant cause of mortality, especially among children. The most commonly performed surgery on children was the tracheotomy where the windpipe was opened to prevent death from suffocation from the dreaded complications of diphtheria, which was so prevalent among the poor. Tuberculosis ran rampant as did malaria and typhoid fever. Coronary artery disease was almost unheard of, and the occasionally diagnosed case of myocardial infarction was considered a showcase because of its rarity. Today, coronary artery disease in Iran is as prevalent as it is in the western world.

Life had little value, and patient advocacy was non-existent. I remember well the case of a young farmer who had mitral valve stenosis (a narrowing of the valve between the left chambers of the heart) and who was in the hospital to have it repaired. In those days repair meant the doctor enlarged the valve by sticking his index finger through it. The farmer was assigned to a surgeon who operated only on Wednesdays; the rest of the week was devoted to his private practice. The farmer was kept without food and went through the usual pre-operative preparation, including enema, shaving, and pre-op medications etc, every Tuesday in anticipation of surgery the following day. But he was still waiting for his operation when I left my surgical rotation six weeks later.

The freshmen class of the medical school was divided alphabetically into smaller groups to accommodate laboratory experiments and equipment use. Microscopes were shared between two students. My microscope partner turned out to be one of the twelve female students in the class.

I introduced myself as "Fraydoon."

She said, "My name is Maheen."

Maheen was very attractive, green-eyed, and petite with eyes reminiscent of the famous National Geographic photo of Sharbat Gula, the striking Afghan girl, with some Elizabeth Taylor thrown in. Studious and sophisticated, she played piano well and carried herself regally. Her father was one of the country's top lawyers who defended Dr. Mossadegh in his trial after his regime fell. Maheen came to school by way of chauffeured limousine. Our friendship grew gradually during the long medical school years but always maintained its necessary professional distance.

In a class of over two hundred male students who were mostly deprived of social intimacy with the opposite sex, the presence of the twelve female students hardly went unnoticed, especially in Maheen's case. Through no doing of her own, she found herself at the center of attention, and our close professional contact as classmates and then as friends came under close scrutiny and became the stuff of gossip and conjecture.

The sixth and the final year of medical school was meant to give us hands-on practical training in the form of an internship. To my pleasant surprise, Maheen had chosen to serve her internship at the same hospital where I would serve mine.

The year of internship provided plenty of opportunity for us to be together both at work and away, taking our budding relationship beyond the boundaries of platonic classmates. The well-guarded disguise of our mutual attraction melted away. We learned a lot more about each other during the long hours of talks in all odd hours of the day or night, whether in the hospital or out on a discreet date. A deeper level of understanding of her character made her more appealing to me than ever. Our closeness and dedication to each other during the internship was among the top issues of the class rumor mill, and the other students were abuzz with speculations about our "imminent marriage."

I was well aware of her popularity, not only among the twenty-to-one male dominated class, but in society in general. I was familiar with her exceptional attributes, with her work ethic, integrity, wisdom, and social maturity, all of which made her ideal as a life partner. But I was not sure if I wanted to settle down at that point. The Augustinian cry of calling out for chastity but whispering, "But not yet Lord!" resonated within me. As much as I cared for her, something in me rebelled against the idea of long-term commitment and settling down. I wanted to see the world. I knew

I would continue my education abroad but could not clearly see or predict my future enough to justify dragging her along with me. I cared for her, thought about her a great deal, and listened to her favorite record, "La Petite Fleur," which had become symbolic of our relationship since we had heard it together so often. The song always reminded me of her face and the proximity of her presence.

Lying awake in my bed in the early hours of the morning, I got up again and again to replay "La Petite Fleur" on my record player. Through the window of my bedroom I looked outside. The full moon was up high in the cloudless sky, and the world seemed peaceful and quiet. Tochal Summit, with its shrunken summer whitecap, looked radiant with the thin light cast by the moon's silvery rays. From where I stood, I could see the village of Darband where Maheen lived. Earlier that evening, we had driven through the canopied street leading to the top of a hill where we had watched the sun set. We discussed our views about the future and what it may have in store for us.

I was aware of the multitude of the families who had approached hers for Khast Gari, an initial indication of interest on behalf of an eligible bachelor. She told me about these pre-proposals, adding, "I will wait for you as long as you want me to."

With so many knocking at her door and with our graduation approaching, her family demanded an answer from us. The fact of the cultural stigma about a woman remaining unmarried into her twenties added to the pressure. As difficult and painful of a choice as it was, our genuine affection for each other and the desire to maintain our friendship made going our separate ways somewhat easier. We recognized the different patterns of our projected lives at that juncture and decided to follow our individual paths but to depart as the best of friends.

In our final days of internship, Maheen became engaged to a promising young Ph.D., a graduate from Columbia University in the U.S. Well-respected internationally and in the hierarchy of the world's oil business, he was invited back to Iran to join senior management to run the huge Iranian oil industry.

Her marriage turned out to be a happy one. She and her husband Mehdi lived in Tehran where they enjoyed the appealing life that the country offered during the Sixties and early Seventies. Shortly after the Iranian Revolution, they moved to the U.S. where they have lived ever since.

Despite time and distance, Maheen and I remained friends and have stayed in touch over the years.

Maheen has lived alone since the death of her husband from a brain tumor a few years ago. His death was devastating for her. She has tried to fill the void by immersing herself in her busy psychiatric practice. Her successful three sons, who live in different parts of the U.S., remain close to her. Maheen and I talk now and then. During the years of my absence from Iran, she remained in touch with my mother and sister providing them assistance and emotional support in the vacuum that my departure had created.

My long-standing friendship with Maheen ranks high on the list of gifts — from my health to my family — for which I will always remain eternally grateful.

WITH CLASSMATES IN MEDICAL SCHOOL. (ME IN SUNGLASSES)

GRADUATION PARTY (LEFT TO RIGHT: ME, MAHEEN, AND CLASSMATES)

MEDICAL SCHOOL (LEFT TO RIGHT: NAS, ME, AND CLASSMATE)

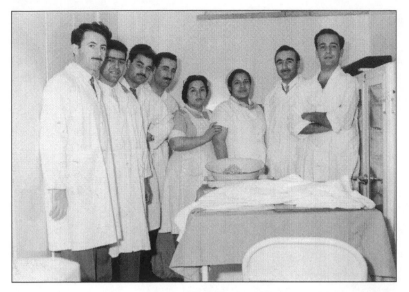

INTERNS WITH OPERATING ROOM STAFF. ALI, SECOND FROM LEFT, ME,
FAR RIGHT

END OF THE INTERNSHIP, MAHEEN AND ME

10. THE HAPPIEST MAN IN THE WORLD

In 1958, during my fourth year of medical school, I decided to build a home for my family. As much as we enjoyed living in the house that we shared with my mother's uncle, we needed a home of our own. My mother felt strongly about it, but my father could not have cared less about owning a home.

As my father and I walked together through the streets of Tehran one day, he pointed to a homeless man. "Baba Joon, you see this man?" I looked over and saw the man under cardboard and some scraps of tin as a roof.

"What about him?" I asked.

My father said, "He could well be one of the happiest men in the world."

In his dusty and tattered clothing, Morshed Khaki did indeed seem happy enough to me. Without romanticizing the scourge of poverty, I knew what my father was saying in the broader philosophical sense. I had experienced the happiness of an ascetic life first-hand living with my grandmother. But that was a distant memory and had faded since I'd tasted the joy of the world of belongings.

Most of the fundamental differences between my parents appeared insurmountable to me, but in this issue of having a home of one's own, I felt I could help.

I understood my mother's unhappiness and sympathized with her concerns. I knew owning a home had been her long-time dream, and I felt obligated to do something about it before leaving the country. With graduation from medical school only a couple of years away, time was running out.

As fortune would have it, the government around this time was offering judges an opportunity to buy some parcels of land in a nice section of town. We cajoled and encouraged my father to exercise his option, and I offered to build a home on the property, assuring him that he did not have to worry about anything else other than paying monthly installments, which he could comfortably afford. He finally agreed, and I purchased the necessary building materials with the financial backing of my mother's family. With the help of my architect friends who designed and supervised the project, our future home began to take shape and was ready for occupancy in just over a year.

The two-story dwelling had copious light, five spacious rooms, two full bathrooms, a large kitchen, and a facade of Italian marble, which was en vogue at the time. We built the house on a gentle hill with a view of the mountain.

We were ready to move, but my mother wouldn't leave, not until we had sacrificed a sheep and gave it to the needy. "For good luck," my mother said.

It was in the middle of summer, and I had a date with Simin that evening.

I drove in the morning to the southern section of the city, where I'd lived as a child. Now an adult, nothing had changed. I drove through the dusty, donkey-filled streets to a location where farmers sold goats, camels, and other assorted pack animals. After the usual haggling about the price and the quality of the man's sheep (about which I knew nothing), I chose one and purchased it.

With some help, I managed to put the poor creature in the back seat of my small car. The smelly, restless beast spent the whole trip baying from the open window at passing cars.

I put on my dark sunglasses and tried to ignore my noisy, unsightly passenger in the back seat. Reaching home, I heaved a sigh of relief and let the sheep out of the car, unaware that the heavier task was ahead. The car, I discovered, was littered with thousands of small, smelly sheep droppings. After meticulous cleaning by hand, I had to use a generous amount of eau de cologne to combat the odor. I opened the windows, hoping that cross-currents would eliminate the horrid smell as I drove later that evening toward my rendezvous with Simin.

Simin's life revolved around exactly three things: Her looks, the latest European fashions, and parties. This was the way of life for the privileged few. Her elaborate hairdo included some silver and platinum streaks. That evening she wore a bizarre dress that flared out mid-thigh and narrowed as it ended above her knees, effectively concealing her sensual, trim, and appealing figure. We drove in my humble-by-comparison car for less recognition into a village and parked on a remote graveled road surrounded by farmland and hills dotted with grazing sheep. Simin's impractical dress, the cramped space of my car, and our eager desire soon found us naked on the ground. Later as I took her back to her own car, I thought I could still discern hints of the earlier sheepish smell mixing with Simin's perfume. Reaching home, however, I could find no traces of the earlier sheep droppings; they'd been replaced with silvery traces of Simin's platinum hair.

11. MAY YOU GROW OLD IN PEACE

For a long time growing up, it felt like I was the only child in our family. Although my brother Manuchehr lived in the same house, my father's stubborn attitude toward him as an unwanted child kept him separate and isolated from the rest of the family. I was deeply saddened and felt bad to see him sitting alone in his room. I was too young to comprehend or figure out any possible reason for this.

The arrival of my sister Mariam brought warmth and coherence into what had become my parents' polarized and tumultuous marriage and mitigated to some degree my unhappiness caused by the unfair manner in which my brother was treated. For the first time, I saw that my father was capable of showing tender emotion. Mariam's birth was a catalyst in giving our family a semblance of a normal, loving family life.

I was eight years old when Mariam was born. I remember the tiny burgundy color marking over her upper lip. According to Persian folklore, such marks were caused by a lunar eclipse or *Mah gereftegi*, during which the expecting mother must have scratched her abdomen in the place corresponding to the baby's affected area.

Mariam excelled from the beginning at school. I watched her perform in a play in the same coed school I had attended several years earlier. I remember how excited she was to play the role of the princess in the final school play opposite Khosro Jahanbani who played the role of the prince who in real life married princess Shahnaz, the oldest daughter of the Shah.

Mariam's high school was a fair distance from the new home I'd had built. I gave her rides as much as I could since her school was on my way to the university. Sometimes when we arrived a bit early, I parked on the street opposite the entrance and waited for her as I soaked up the flirtations of the girls as they passed by, Mariam would tell me about them and about the complimentary things they said about me. I dismissed their childish comments as irrelevant but secretly I loved every second of it. Some of the older girls called me on the phone and giggled until I hung up. I met others at parties, and, although they fueled my vanity and my desire, I remained politely aloof knowing that my world and theirs could never mix.

Life was especially difficult for my sister and her young female friends. While some women in Iran accepted their limitations as the established social norm, the more ambitious women felt boxed in, unable to find opportunities to grow. It was a sad reality to see so many individuals like my sister, girls and women with tremendous desire and potential, unable to develop their god-given talents.

Mariam was always at the top of her class, enthusiastic about life, full of energy, and eager for personal growth. She looked up to me, appreciative and envious of the freedom I enjoyed in conducting my own life. I know she would have done equally well if not better, if she had been given the same freedom and opportunities as a woman that I enjoyed as a man.

Life in those days was good in Tehran. The decades had the conveniences of the modern world and the charm and slow pace of the old. Yes, there were frustrations. I grew annoyed with the injustices of the corrupt system, with the mentality of a population that continued to tolerate that system, and with the growing irreconcilable differences between my parents. But in balance, my life as a young man in Tehran was quite pleasant.

The increasingly unhappy marriage of my parents continued as long as I lived in Iran but soon after my departure, their marriage finally fell apart.

By now, over sixty-years-old, my father married a young girl, the same age as his own daughter. She was an eighteen-year-old from a poor peasant family with no education.

Mariam was close to graduation from high school just as I was preparing to leave the country for my post-graduate training. She was an attractive seventeen-year-old. Her looks, personality, and intelligence made her a desirable woman, eligible for a suitable and serious mate of the highest caliber. Before I left the country in the late Fifties, a powerful army officer who had seen Mariam in the Army Officer's Club with my uncle expressed his desire to marry her.

He was brought up as a young man with the Shah and had gone to military academy with him and then to Switzerland to study. He remained the Shah's closest aid and confidante and was perhaps among the most powerful man next to the monarch during the twenty-five years that he ruled the country. Through my uncle, he had asked if he could approach my father and ask for Mariam's hand.

When my uncle presented this message, my father flew into a rage. He felt the man was much too old (the man was in his fifties) and that his reputation, like most of those associated with the royal court, was tainted. The irony was that my father himself at the age of sixty had hypocritically married someone Mariam's age.

Mariam, recently graduated from high school and living with my parents, bore the brunt of the emotional turmoil created by my father's selfish behavior.

Shortly after my arrival in England in 1961, I was informed about Mariam's engagement and her impending marriage. I learned that the man she was engaged to had been educated in the United States and came from a family with considerable wealth. But as it turned out, he was a socially gauche eccentric and miserly intellectual who could not hold a meaningful job. Their marriage was not a happy one, and it ended in divorce.

My mother, having experienced a rather disappointing married life herself, encouraged Mariam to continue her education while she took on the responsibilities of raising Mariam's two young sons.

Mariam obtained her M.B.A from Tehran University and graduated at the top of her class with accolades and began her career at the National Iranian Oil Company, where, through her usual diligence and enthusiasm, she rose through the ranks. Recognizing the value of her work in dealing with the contracts of the foreign oil companies, she was among a handful of women that the patriarchal system of the Islamic Revolution could not afford to lose. She found working within the system difficult and frustrating, but she endured.

Mariam remains bitter about her failed marriage and points to the circumstances that pushed her into it so soon after graduation from high school. With the separation of our parents and my absence from the country, her support system had disintegrated.

Mariam is one of the few in our family who continues to live in Iran. Most of our family, including her two sons, live in the U.S. The older son Nader graduated from Perdue's engineering program and works for GM. Kambiz, Mariam's youngest, is a physician on the faculty at UCLA. Mariam stayed in the old country mostly because of her devotion to our mother who died peacefully in her nineties from natural causes. Her devotion to my mother, her responsible position at work and strong support system of a group of intellectuals friends, architects, painters, and writers has given her life some balance in a society that otherwise tends to subjugate women.

I have learned that my father's new marriage produced four children, three boys and a girl, most barely older than my own children.

I am told that my father's final years were not pleasant. He was abused by his young wife and the children who squeezed him for his last penny, demanding more and more from him. He was lonely and neglected.

On a snowy day, while coming back from his office, he fell and broke his hip. He was taken to the city hospital where indigents were cared for and where he died shortly after as the result of complications from surgery.

My mother and sister learned about his death months later through my brother Manuchehr who had accidentally learned about it from a complete stranger. I was profoundly saddened by the news and appalled by the circumstances of my father's death. I could only hope that his inclination for anonymity and his lack of interest in the materialistic world were a source of comfort to him as he faced the final years of his life.

It saddens me to think that a man with so much potential squandered the dignity, prestige, and well-being of his old age, a phase of life so precious, especially in Iranian culture where people commonly wish each other well by saying, "I hope your old days will be peaceful and filled with respect." His were neither.

Mariam and Manuchehr found his burial site unmarked. They provided a proper site for him.

I heard that my father's oldest boy from the last wife joined the army. The daughter married and lived in Tehran for a while. I also heard that the whole family left the country shortly after the Iranian Revolution and settled in Sweden, although I have not been able to substantiate any of this. Still, I know I have four young half-brothers and a half-sister somewhere in the world. I wish them well and hope that my father's strong belief and faith in the potential of his children will help to see them through.

12. OFF FOR ENGLAND

My long-held desire to see the outside world was finally coming to fruition, and I could not be happier.

The long journey of studying had prepared me for the first phase of my profession, but to become a specialist in a particular field, I needed to get further post-graduate training in the western world as I had always planned to do.

To help my finances, I worked as an on call physician covering the night shift in a rubber company for six months.

I sold my loyal but beat-up V.W. and asked my mother, knowing how little she cared for dogs, if she wouldn't mind taking care of my black poodle. Picky. I was twenty-five when I left Tehran for London with little money, no place to live or to stay, and no job.

On the day of my departure, relatives and friends showed up in Mehr Abad airport to say farewell. In the final minutes before my flight was to leave, my aunt Shamsi gave me some *lavashak* (a thinly-rolled, dried fruit) and asked me to pass it along to a friend of hers in London. Not happy with such a last-minute request, I stuffed the snacks into my carry-on bag. When my plane touched down at last in London, the customs officers demanded to know the nature of this unusual-looking food in my bag. They thought it might be opium.

"No, no!" I explained in the best English I could manage. "Not opium. Good to eat." To convince him, I tore off a strip of the dried fruit, chewed it up, and swallowed it down. Mollified at last, the customs agent said, "All right" and sent me on my way.

My primary objective during the first few months of my stay in London was to strengthen my command of the English language before finding a suitable position for post-graduate training. I had to find a position soon and before my limited funding ran out. This was a source of concern. Financially, I couldn't support myself for more than a few months.

Nas and a few other classmates who were already in England helped me rent a room on Kensington Street. I wound up within a short walking distance of the Earls Court subway station where most foreign students lived at the time.

The small room was on the third floor of a large Victorian building. The only source of light for the L-shaped room was a narrow, nearly-opaque window overlooking Kensington Street.

The proprietor was a woman in her sixties. She lived with her forty-year-old flamboyantly homosexual son on the first floor. She was morbidly obese and never left her lazy-boy chair. I could count on one hand the number of times I actually saw her standing up. Her chair was strategically placed at a spot by the bay window where she could monitor the comings and goings of the tenants. She had stiff purple hair that matched the unhealthy color of her face. Her presence behind the bay window was a helpful land marker for me and helped me to pick out which house of the many look-alikes on the row was mine.

My room was the smallest on the third floor. The other two rooms were occupied by two night club dancers.

I seldom saw my two neighbors for the first few weeks since they returned from work after midnight and slept late during the day.

Maureen, a shapely brunette in her late twenties, was the taller of the two. Despite our proximity as neighbors, she remained a nearly invisible presence. Her red-haired freckle-faced friend, whose name escapes me now, was bubbly and more friendly.

Shortly after my arrival, I started language classes, which took a few hours out of each day and left me with plenty of time to wander the city on foot or by public transport. Along the way, I did some exploring and got to know the city reasonably well.

The opacity of the window that jealously guarded against England's anemic light kept my L-shaped room gray all the time. With winter approaching, my room, especially in the evenings, became cold and damp. A stubborn, coin-operated electric heater served as my sole source of heat. I had to have a stack of shillings ready by my bedside to satisfy the demanding heater throughout the night. The cold and lonely evenings of the first few months finally warmed as Maureen came out of her shell and began to join me in my room when she returned home from work after a late night of professional dancing.

I am not quite sure who initiated calling me by new name, but I know it took its root in the Kensington house. I remember Maureen, late at night and with her face still adorned with make-up and glitter, calling me "Fero."

Though our bodies understood each other well, her narrow perception of the world and my limited command of English made for superficial talks, leaving me with many unanswered questions from the practical to the philosophical.

Who was she? What was her understanding of a man she called Fero who eagerly waited for her in a small L-shaped room of a Victorian house on Kensington Street? She knew I was a doctor looking for post-graduate training, and I knew that she danced with a group of show girls in a Cabaret. We didn't always understand each other, but we didn't always have to. Our relationship remained grounded in the present tense, and neither one of us focused in any way on the future.

At the beginning, my nickname in the Kensington house rang awkwardly in my ears, especially when I introduced myself to people. The name "Fero" left me feeling like an impostor. It took some time to overcome the feeling, which I finally managed once my Persian friends from back home began using it. I finally adopted it in the 1970s as part of my legal name.

With my limited funds depleting fast, I began sending applications to hospitals inquiring about positions in post-graduate training.

A few months passed, and I was down to my last few pounds when I received an invitation for an interview from Port-Talbot General Hospital, a hospital in a small industrial town in South Wales.

I was elated to learn at the end of the interview that I had an excellent chance of obtaining the position of Senior House Surgeon. I celebrated the occasion in the nearest pub with the very last of my money.

It never occurred to me what I would do if I could not secure a post-graduate position in England. I thought of this possibility only retrospectively when Ali, another classmate facing a similar situation and unable to find a position said to me, "Truly amazing to be able to strike out like that. To throw yourself into the unknown and uncharted waters and have enough trust in yourself that you would not drown."

To me it came down to the simple act of sink or swim. I could not convince him, though. I knew he thought of me as a risk-taker. Ali needed a firmer and more secure ground. I stayed in England; he went back to Iran.

My new position provided me with a room in the hospital as well as meals plus a reasonable monthly salary.

The challenges of my daily responsibilities in the hospital kept me so busy I didn't have time to be bored. While the rest of the town drank and watched rugby, I worked.

With a regular paycheck coming in, I bought a Ford Anglia and settled as best as I could in my relatively rustic lodgings located between the two more cosmopolitan cities of Cardiff and Swansea.

The challenges of my work kept me mostly in the hospital. I worked with two consultant surgeons: a nondescript, conservative, middle-aged man named Mr. Bowen and a much younger Mr. Howard Jones who was warm, flashy, and full of positive energy.

Mr. Jones was a competent surgeon with excellent credentials and had been trained in top British medical institutions. He had sandy blond hair, blue eyes, bushy eyebrows, and a warm, friendly smile. He also had a reputation for being fun-loving and mischievous.

In a medical meeting where I was seated next to him, when the female keynote speaker, a world renowned liver specialist from London, in her opening remarks acknowledged Mr. Jones's presence in the audience, he turned to me and whispered, "She and I were classmates in medical school. She still remembers when I took her panties off on graduation day."

Both Mr. Jones and Mr. Bowen were based in Swansea but conducted clinics and operated on certain days at our hospital. (The surgeons who become Fellows of Royal College of Surgeon, are addressed as Mr.)

The bulk of responsibility and around-the-clock dealings with surgical problems, however, were handled by me and by an Indian doctor named Dr. Sabir, who as the surgical registrar, wss my immediate supervisor.

Dr. Sabir, a middle aged-man, had lived in the area forever. And, like many other foreign registrars, was an unlikely candidate to climb up the last rung of the ladder to become a consultant. He was an average-sized, ebony-colored man with large, black eyes set apart frog-like, creating an aura of extreme alertness and acute peripheral vision. When this was combined with his ever-present smirk, we were often left with the impression that he had transcended the world of the ordinary and was in perpetual amusement of what he saw beyond. He had an uncompromising British manner, a characteristic not uncommon among educated Indians of the post-colonial era. He seemed more British at times than the British.

My contract with the hospital was for one year, during which I learned a good deal about the practical aspects of surgery by participating in daily patient care, attending clinics, and assisting in the operating room.

My limited social activities were confined to driving around the countryside with young women, mostly local nurses. Occasionally I visited another medical school classmate named Zia who worked as a house surgeon in orthopedic surgery in Swansea about an hour away. He had arrived in England six months ahead of me and seemed settled in with a much better command of the language than I had. A bit of a daredevil, he was an outstanding skier in Iran. He drove his recently-purchased TR4 like a madman.

British law in the Sixties permitted foreigners a grace period of six months during which they could drive with their own driver's licenses, after which they had to obtain the British driver's license. I was driving with my Persian driver's license during this grace period when I was pulled over by a cop.

The officer stepped out of his green MG, marched up to my window, and demanded to see my license.

"I have been in this country not quite six months yet," I said, "and have already applied for a British license."

He looked at my Iranian license – with no picture and printed entirely in Farsi – and then turned it upside down in an apparent attempt to decipher the unfamiliar hieroglyphs. With a puzzled squint and the self-satisfied authority of a Persian scholar, he said, "Thank you sir, have a good day."

He went on his way, and I went on mine.

I was getting restless with local dates and cultural provincialism limited to drinking in the pubs and watching the rugby matches with the neighboring towns during the weekends. In search of more cosmopolitan and sophisticated companionship, I was briefly drawn to a college girl whom I had met in the clinic where she had been accompanying her parents.

She and I dated twice, and shortly after, she returned to Bath where she was enrolled in college. Deeply infatuated, I could not keep her out of my mind. Without informing her, I decided to visit her in Bath. I set out and reached the city before midnight. The city was unsightly, full of black Dickensian Victorian buildings that even the silvery light of the full moon could not improve. My impulsive drive to see her came to nothing since she wasn't home. Soon, my infatuation was over as quickly as it had started.

Nights with a full moon, like the night I made my fruitless trek to Bath, had an intoxicating effect on me. They made me more romantic, idealistic, and adventurous. The full moon enhanced my temperament and made me a Utopian dreamer.

I remember a character in an Italian comic movie who would go so crazy in a full moon that he had to be chained in the cellar where he howled like wolf all night long. I was not quite that bad, but close.

Many of my impulses during such evenings bordered on irrational behavior, such as the time back in Iran when I called Ali to join me in a midnight winter drive over the dangerous snow-covered passes of the Alborz mountains. He thought I was out of my mind, but I wanted to see the reflection of the moonlight on the Caspian Sea, and I don't think anything could have stopped me.

Or, another time in the summer, when the moon was full and low, I sped like a maniac along the sharp switch-backs of winding roads carved into the side of the mountain before losing control and overturning the car. With the help of other drivers who stopped for me, I put the warped but still-running VW beetle on its wheels and continued, battered and bruised but invigorated, toward my next rendezvous.

In England, Port Talbot grew smaller very fast, and I was eager to move on to a bigger city and a more challenging position.

In response to my inquiry from different hospitals, I received an acceptance from a reputable multi-disciplinary institution affiliated with London University. I was hired as Senior House Surgeon at Old Church Hospital in Rumford, which covered a large area of London's suburbs. I took my place as a junior member of one of the three rotating surgical teams.

As a house surgeon, I worked with an easy-going Australian registrar named Jack Calendar. Each team was under the direction of a separate surgical consultant. A thoracic surgeon named Mr. Park led my team.

Short, bald, and rigidly serious, Mr. Park wore black-rimmed glasses, never smiled, and drove a classic black Rolls-Royce. He was barely visible behind the wheel of that monstrous car.

I was assigned a room in the house-staff quarters next to the dormitory of a large school of nurses, most of whom came from Ireland.

In addition to our individual bedrooms, we shared a spacious dining room with a massive table with white table cloths, comfortable leather chairs, and well-polished silverware. We dined on mediocre British cuisine in a formal and somber setting. In the lounge, we had a bar full of beer that the house staff used on the honor system. Every morning around six o'clock, the maids served us tea or coffee in bed. After a routine breakfast of eggs and salty bacon with toast and orange marmalade, we started our rounds at the hospital.

For recreation, there were four well-groomed grass tennis courts, and I started playing tennis again. Though London was only thirty minutes away by car, I hardly went to the city except for special occasions.

This was 1962, and the British National Health Care System was in its infancy. In order to deal with the limitations of resources, the British Government had established a strict program of rationing. For example, the determination of the concentration of blood potassium, a rather important test for certain more complex medical conditions, was rationed because of its cost at the time. We were allowed to order it only so many times during the twenty-four hours our team was responsible for emergency admissions. We had to be prudent, utilizing the test discreetly for those who needed it most.

The same was true for elective surgery. The elective surgical schedules were made the night before with some provisions allowing for emergencies. If such emergencies exceeded our expectations, as they often did, then the elective cases would be postponed. Because of this continued bottlenecking, the waiting period for many elective surgeries increased beyond the threshold of tolerance for most American patients. At the time it seemed that the British patients accepted the guidance of the physicians without question. I would discover over time that in the United States, patients demanded more autonomy and played a more active and participatory role in the decision-making process. They were also more inclined to sue when things didn't go exactly as planned.

Another example of the trial and error of the British health system in the early Sixties involved the guidelines mandating that anyone who was checked out of the emergency room and for whatever reason was unable to go home safely, had to be provided with an ambulance at hospital expense for their return home. As one of the casualty officers, I ordered ambulances for many people of all ages who had spent their last shilling in the pubs and came to the emergency room drunk, demanding to be sent home by ambulance. After a while and because of such abuse, the guidelines changed, requiring the payment of a couple of shillings for the visit to the emergency room, which dramatically decreased the wasteful demand on our ambulance services.

Despite an environment of professionalism and shared resources, a strict hierarchy existed at the hospital. One could identify the pecking order among the nurses by their uniforms. The head nurses, called "Sisters," wore blue uniforms and head gear more like nuns with starched wrist cuffs and little if any make-up. They were responsible for a great deal of clinical and direct patient care, and they assigned certain responsibilities to others on the nursing staff. As stiff and somber as the working atmosphere was, beyond the walls of the patients ward, it was a different story.

The house staff's living quarters, with its well-stocked bar and good collection of records, was the site of frequent parties attended mostly by nurses, many of whom, once they let their hair down, could be both funny and frisky.

One day I was assigned to be second assistant during a major thoracic surgery performed by Mr. Park and first-assisted by Jack, my registrar. My responsibility was to provide a better exposure by retracting the tissues away from the operating field. I should note that our operating scrubs at the time were a bit peculiar. The trousers did not have any waist-band to hold them up, and we often had to cut a piece of gauze to use as a belt. I am not sure whether this was part of the national health policy or unique to our hospital. An hour or so into the operation, I felt someone behind me. That by itself was not unusual since nurses often came close to the surgical field to see what was going on. But when I felt the pressure of a hand against the small of my back and heard the snip of scissors, I knew I was in trouble. A nurse had cut my gauze belt! Pressing myself against the table, I managed to keep my pants up as the nurses giggled behind me. Ten minutes passed. Then Mr. Park asked me to go to the other side of the table to retract a new area. Noticing me shuffling with my pants nearly down to my knees, he started laughing for what I suspect may have been the first time in his rigid British life.

Pranks against the house-staff plotted by the nurses were common, especially in the holiday season during which all the wards were decorated and a great deal of partying went on. During this period, it was customary to pay a visit to each ward and, over a glass of port, socialize with the nursing staff. When I went to my room, well after midnight during the Christmas Holiday to rest, I noticed that my mattress had vanished and my room had been ransacked. Calling the supervisor to see if they could fix my room, I learned from her that this was a prank commonly practiced by the nurses during the holidays. She suggested perhaps I could sleep in a bed in one of the wards since half of them were empty. I chose an empty ward and wasn't quite sleeping when I heard the twitters of the nurses as they crept toward my bed. In the dim light, I could barely make them out, but what they were carrying as they made their way toward me – a rectal exam tray – was clear as day. I jumped out of bed and started running in my boxer shorts down the corridor with the gang of giggling nurses in hot pursuit.

In 1962, England suffered through a terrible winter. The smog and fog were so thick and hazardous, especially for the elderly and debilitated, that the public was repeatedly advised to stay indoors. The visibility was so poor that I saw many individuals in the emergency room who had injuries resulting from walking, perfectly sober but blinded by the fog, into trees or lamp-posts.

The weather affected me. I missed the Persian sun and the mountains and the beauty of my home country.

In many ways, England had lost its charm; I felt miserable and began just going through the motions at work. I was fatigued, anorexic, depressed, and had bouts of anxiety for months. My pulse quickened, large lymph nodes began to appear on my neck, and I found myself perpetually exhausted. Although I strongly suspected infectious mononucleosis, it could not be confirmed by the usual blood test, and a cervical node biopsy didn't offer a conclusive diagnosis either.

I was convinced I had some sinister and deadly disease. I decided if the prognosis proved to be as bleak as I thought, I would face the inevitable in some form of a lethal accident in the high alpine country. I had a car and enough money to take me to the Swiss Alps.

Besides, I was not happy with the post-graduate training in England. My unhappiness stemmed from the fact that the graduates of such programs did not receive adequate practical experience. Under the British system, one could have qualified for the Fellowship of the Royal College of Surgeons without having much practical surgical experience, although a rigorous theoretical test was required. Under the American system, candidates had to go through systematic surgical training before becoming eligible for the equally rigorous theoretical examination in order to become a Diplomat of the American Board of Surgery.

To become a surgical consultant also seemed much more difficult in England. I had seen too many registrars in their mid-fifties still patiently waiting to climb up this last rung of the ladder.

I decided not to renew my contract with the hospital. Instead I took a temporary job as the director of a couple of nursing homes in the London suburbs where I replaced an older physician who would be on vacation for a couple of months. I moved into his well-furnished and well-stocked two bedroom apartment. A chauffeured car ferried me to and from the nursing homes for my daily rounds.

My responsibilities turned out to be far less challenging than I had anticipated or than I had experienced before. That left me time to study for the upcoming Educational Council for Foreign Medical Graduates (ECFMG) exam, which I needed to pass in order to apply for post-graduate training in the U.S.

I took the test in London and passed with flying colors.

Pt. III – Coming to America

13. YEARNING TO BREATHE FREE

During the 1960s, a shortage of manpower in the U.S. led to a crisis in the delivery of adequate health care. There was an across-the-board need for health care providers and especially for medical doctors. Consequently, newly founded medical schools proliferated throughout the country, and foreign medical school graduates were enticed to continue their post-graduate training in the United States.

This was considered a win-win solution for both the donor and the recipient countries: The U.S. would get an influx of doctors whose cost of education had been paid by their respective countries. In return, foreign doctors would acquire the expertise of the latest advances in medicine, an expertise they would then bring with them back to their countries of origin.

The assumption in part, however, was flawed. As it turned out, most of the doctors, after finishing their post-graduate training, for a variety of reasons, stayed in the U.S. and only a scant few trickled back.

The net result was a significant brain drain from some of the poorest nations that could least afford to lose their best and brightest. This was especially noticeable during the Sixties among the graduates of Tehran Medical School, where over 50% of the graduates of my class, for instance, came to the United States and where most are still practicing today.

In response, many developing nations, through rapid proliferation of second rate medical schools, created a surplus of poorly educated doctors, most without jobs in their own country. And in the U.S., the increased numbers of graduates from the new medical schools caught up with the demand for the most part, although in some areas the shortage still remains a problem.

To secure a position in an approved residency program in the U.S., I needed a year of internship in the States and since there was no reciprocity between the British and the American medical systems, I could not get any credit for my two years of training in England. To fulfill this requirement, I chose a small community hospital in a Chicago suburb to do my internship.

In the final weeks of June 1963, I sold my Ford Anglia, packed my few possessions, and left London for Southampton to cross the Atlantic by way of the Queen Mary luxury liner.

The ocean-liner was making one of her last transatlantic crossings before retiring as a tourist center in California. The Queen Mary carried a special aura for so many in that era. It had been the centerpiece of many romantic novels, movies, and storied adventures. The fact that she would soon be retired made the voyage across the Atlantic all the more appealing.

On board, a narrow bed took up half of my small economy cabin. A round, window provided the only source of light, which streaked into the room in pale, gray shafts. I could hear the foamy green ocean water rolling up against the ship's steel hull and the ever-present monotonous thrum of the liner's massive engines. I dumped my luggage in my chicken-coop of a cabin and vowed to spend as little time there as possible.

Instead I spent most of the trip in the exhilarating, sunny or moon-lit salty air of the open decks above. Sumptuous dinners were served in an elegant, wood-paneled ballroom, where a full orchestra played in the evenings, and folks tried to dance against the motion of the ship. And if the rocking ship didn't throw of their equilibrium, the mass consumption of the kitchen's excellent wines certainly would.

Although I drank and socialized and danced with a young lady from California, I spent most of the week-long journey lying out on the upper deck where I'd lose myself in the expansive starry sky. Hypnotized by the fiery sunrises and later by the enormous shimmering moon, I reflected back on my life as a child, lying in that same way – stretched out, fingers interlaced behind my head – on the roof of our small house in Persia and making the same optimistic wishes. I felt like I'd come a long way from those dreamy, fantasy-filled days. In a way, though, in a very profound way, I hadn't gone anywhere at all.

But by far the most lasting memory of this voyage is the radical transformation of my outlook and changed-perception of my surroundings as I approached the American shores.

From a very young age, the United States had captivated my imagination, as it did for countless youth throughout the world. America's dazzling natural beauty fascinated me. As a youngster I looked for hours at the photographs of the mountains, shores, deserts, and vast prairies of this blessed country, wondering if I could see it someday and maybe climb some of its mountains. Later, as my political awareness grew, I came to admire above all the country's liberal and democratic constitution. To me it represented the breeding ground for the idealism of mankind where everyone could realize his or her potential.

The opaque veil that so insidiously had warped my view of the world during the latter part of my stay in England and which had made everything dull, insipid, and without meaning, evaporated as I approached the shores of the United States.

I felt intuitively certain of the bright future this New World had in store for me.

On a hot July afternoon, as the Queen Mary approached New York harbor close to the Statue of Liberty – the symbol that I had seen so often and that had loomed so large in my mind – my heart raced.

As if in a dream, full of the lingering experiences of the Atlantic crossing, I stepped onto the sizzling streets of New York City. Due to a lack of sleep during the crossing, my mind registered little from the city other than the sight of a heavy policeman with a protruding belly who carried his conspicuous handgun in a holster swinging from his side, a sharp contrast with the police in England where they wore white gloves and carried whistles. The American police officer reminded me of men in cowboy movies.

I needed to sleep. The moment I reached my hotel, I slept and woke up late the following day shortly before my flight was scheduled to leave for Chicago.

I was to report for duty on July 1 at West Suburban Hospital in Oak Park, Illinois. A new man at a new job in a new land. I didn't know what would happen, but I knew for sure I'd make the most of it.

14. YOU'VE NEVER HAD PIZZA?

A tranquil, safe, and affluent community, the village of Oak Park took pride in being the birthplace of Frank Lloyd Wright and the place where Ernest Hemingway grew up and where his father practiced medicine.

Oak Park was also the original home of Sam Giancana, the notorious head of a prominent Mafia family. Giancana lived in a sprawling mansion a couple blocks from the hospital. Many believed his presence was the major reason for Oak Park's extraordinary safety in and around an area otherwise prone to crime. At the time, it was reasonable to assume that cars parked on the Oak Park side of Austin Boulevard, which divided the city from the village and where the hospital was located, would be safe, whereas parking a car on the Chicago side could be quite risky. During the prolonged strike of the garbage collectors, some clever folks put their garbage in gift-wrapped packages and left them in their cars on the Chicago side, knowing the "trash packages" had a good chance of being stolen over night.

The weather in this cold and windy city was quite an improvement over the dreary gray of England. To witness the sunrise as often as I did in Chicago, albeit from the top floors of the hospital and during working hours, was wonderful. I missed sunshine. After all, I had come from a land where the sun was worshiped for centuries by my Zoroastrian ancestors.

I spent most of my time in the hospital, slave to a demanding internship. When on call, I worked throughout the night and continued to work the following day until dusk. Working for thirty-six hours with little or no sleep was not unusual.

On average I had three nights per week and two weekends per month to sleep without interruption. That would have been sufficient if not for the seduction of the sun, the shores of Lake Michigan, and a beautiful blond who loved to drive her convertible MG through the pristine country side of neighboring Wisconsin.

I met Judy, a nurse, late one evening during the early days of my internship when I was called to evaluate a patient under her care. As I entered the room, she was seated behind her desk, fully absorbed in reviewing the patient's chart. On her desk was an electric fan rotating with much fuss and noise. Judy's luxuriant blonde hair was pulled back under her nursing cap with a few strands moving gently against her face. Her fitted white uniform complemented her pleasing figure.

As I entered the room, she stood up and said, "You must be new," and began to report her concerns about the patient.

She was tall with pale green eyes, warm and expressive. She had shallow dimples, a smooth face, and a radiant smile. Best of all, she blushed when she spoke to me.

I noticed the diamond ring on her finger. I found out later, however, that she was unhappy with her engagement and was ready to end it.

During my year in Chicago, I dated Judy and spent as much of my little free time with her as I possibly could.

Recently graduated, she lived in the nursing school next door to the hospital where I lived. We looked forward with much anticipation to our weekends away from work.

In her red convertible, we raced out of Chicago on warm summer days toward neighboring Wisconsin with neither plan nor destination. We turned down any road that seemed picturesque, less traveled, or that caught our fancy. She often wore a black and gold silk scarf over her thick blonde hair. With the strong winds and the thrum of the engine, we couldn't talk much during our drives, but we communicated by our presence and by our proximity.

On one of our weekend excursions, she wore a low-cut, sleeveless, peach-colored dress. I couldn't stop looking at her. She returned my frequent glances with a smile and those charming dimples. Our gaze revealed our desire. I pulled the car over and held her in my arms. Her soft skin was cooled by the fresh summer breeze and enhanced by her Jasmine-scented perfume.

She whispered, "Fraydoon I love you so much."

As I kissed her, she closed her eyes. Her face reflected my own sense of peace and pleasure.

We continued our drive along the vast golden wheat fields in the countryside dotted with myriad pristine lakes and looked around for a more secluded area for the opportunity of a longer embrace. We witnessed some of the most spectacular sunsets in the pastoral setting of this beautiful state where the air scented of wildflowers. Bales of hay speckled the expansive fields under the colorful horizon and the red setting sun.

Our romance was a rich source of bright and vibrant color, which imbued the prism of our world and made the most mundane and ordinary events a delightful experience.

Newly graduated, Judy worked full-time with a demanding schedule almost as hard as mine. The hospital provided my boarding and lodging plus an annual stipend of $2,400, enough to buy a new Corvair.

As long as Judy and I were together, We didn't need anything else. I think she found my accent and my naiveté about American English and customs to be endearing.

Though English was part of the high school curriculum in Iran, we learned the medical terminology in French since the faculty of the medical school comprised mostly French graduates. But it was in England where I really learned conversational English as well as English-language medical terminology.

The variations in terminology between the American and British versions of English created some embarrassing moments in my earlier days in Chicago.

A few weeks after arriving in Chicago, I saw a patient for evaluation of an abdominal pain. After an examination and a proper work-up, I made the diagnosis of an intestinal obstruction and told the young nurse in charge of the ER, "Sister, this patient is very sick and needs to go to the theater." The nurse was puzzled, perhaps alarmed, wondering, how I could advise such a patient to go to a show! Calling her Sister (as we addressed all the nurses in England,) was not helpful either. Was I some religious freak?

It did not take me long to remedy the situation, making my point clear that the patient needed urgent surgery and needed to get to the operating room.

Gradually and over many years I lost my unmistakable English accent and find it surprising to hear that now and then traces of it are still detected by some people.

When it comes to accents, I am not quite sure where I fit. During my periodic travels back to Iran, in order to visit my elderly mother when she could no longer travel to the States, I was often reminded of my thick Farsi accent. I would indeed find it difficult to communicate effectively beyond the mundane and ordinary conversation. And then again, in the United States, where I have spent the past forty five years of my adult life, my accent remains apparent to most people.

Judy loved my accent. She called it "sophisticated and charming." And, although it embarrassed me, she also loved my ignorance about certain elements of American culture. And not just the language blunders or my confusion about American popular culture either.

"You've never had pizza?" she asked one day.

I told her, "No. Never."

"How could you have never had pizza?"

I told her for the same reason she had never had *khoresht-e fesenjan.*

"What is *khoresht-e fesenjan?*" she asked. (She pronounced it like she had a bee sting on her tongue.)

I explained that *khoresht-e fesenjan* is a thick stew made with pomegranate juice, ground fresh walnuts, and chicken or duck.

"Sounds good," she said.

"It's delicious," I insisted. "I can't imagine this famous American pizza of yours can even come close."

She smiled. "We'll see about that."

The next weekend, Judy and I drove to a pizza place I had passed dozens of times but had never entered. Leading me by the hand, she marched us over to a table, sat us down, and instructed the waiter to "give us the works."

Fifteen minutes later, I sat before a large, round tray of the most fragrant and tantalizing food I'd ever seen. Steam rose from the pizza like mist off the summit of Damavand. To my surprise and to Judy's triumphant delight, the pizza tasted even better than it appeared, and after a single slice, I was hooked. Pizza remains among my favorite treats to this day.

Food seemed to play an important role in American culture. Among the major highlights in my medical meetings, were always conversations about the best places to eat. And the American portions were enormous. The smallest ice cream cone was four times bigger than its European counterpart. Soft drinks and coffee were served in cups that looked to me more like milk buckets. And obesity ran rampant, almost in epidemic proportions, even among the children. Also, Americans ate fast. I never got used to that and always finished last when dining with a group.

Conversations about the weather were as prevalent as those about food. So much talk about the weather and forecasting seemed pointless to me. After all, I had come from a country where the sun always shone and where seasons were predictably delineated. However, it did not take long to realize the importance of weather forecasts, particularly around the great lakes area where one could experience all four seasons within a day or two. The old joke about Chicago is true: "If you don't like the weather, just wait an hour, and it will change."

Between the busy schedule of my work and the time I spent with Judy on my days off, there was no room for anything else. I hardly visited my old friend Nas who was doing his orthopedic residency on the other side of town and was planning to get married soon to a woman named Barbara. Nas and his brother Massoud, who was visiting him at the time, invited me and Judy over and prepared *khoresht-e fesenjan* for dinner. Judy loved it.

"Is it your favorite?" she asked me,

"No," I said. "My favorite is *khoresh ghormehsabzi*."

"What is that?"

Nas, and I tried to explain to her the ingredients, among them chives, fenugreek, parsley, sun-dried key lime, and other herbs whose English names we didn't know. We talked about the diet in Iran and the importance of fresh vegetables, rice, and bread as the main staples and our minimal consumption of meat or dessert.

Judy asked, "You didn't eat dessert in Iran?"

I said, "No. Not like here. Fresh fruits and tea are traditionally served after dinner."

I think that disappointed her.

Barbara and Nas married a few weeks later. The small wedding party of the bride and groom, his brother, Judy and I, sat for a long time in a large waiting room in City Hall where the ceremony was to take place. We saw couples of all sizes, shapes, and varieties of accents taking their vows in front of the judge. We waited for a long time until the room was almost empty. Finally, Nas and Barbara were called up. The marriage ritual in front of the bored and tired judge was over in a few minutes. Afterward we went to a Chinese restaurant a few blocks away for dinner.

15. SUCH A NATURAL BEAUTY

Time passed quickly, and, before I knew it, I had to find a position for post-graduate training. I wanted an established university with a residency program that carried weight and recognition in Iran where I was planning to return.

As strongly as I felt about coming to the United States, the ever-present force of gravity from the old country kept pulling me back.

I was restless and lured between the pull of the two cultures. I vacillated over and struggled with this dilemma for a long time. I missed the slow pace of the Persian life, the crowing of the roosters in the countryside, the snowcapped mountains, and the softer blue of the Persian sky. I missed my strong family ties and the support of my large circle of friends. But more importantly, I knew there were people back home who desperately needed the expertise and medical knowledge that I was getting in the States. And yet, during visits to Iran, which I took every couple of years, after a month or so, I could not wait to get back to the U.S.

I suppose that such psychological polarization, tugging at the heart by the two opposing cultures, is not uncommon among first generations of immigrants.

The intensity of this tug-of-war, which varies in each individual, determines the degree of assimilation into the new culture. Those who voluntarily leave their native land seem to have an easier time assimilating than those who have been forced to leave. The latter often create the microcosm of the old culture in their adopted country.

While I believe it is important for the new immigrant to be diligent in assimilating into the new culture, I cannot fathom the attitude of some, who by embracing the new, deny their past completely. How could one build a present and a future without the foundation of those formative earlier years?

The strength of America as an immigrant nation, I believe, stems in no small part from the common embrace of a common ideal and the successful coexistence of the old ways and the new.

For me, the social and political upheaval that later transformed Iran into a significantly different place, made it much easier to put it out of my mind. The newly formed country of the Islamic Republic of Iran was a foreign land to me, where I could rarely if ever find traces of the old, familiar past. I felt like a stranger in my birth place. The Iran I knew was no longer there. I no longer dreamed in Persian.

More entrenched now in American life, I focused my attention on my career.

In response to my inquiries to different universities and medical centers, I received several acceptances for residency programs, among them, the State University of New York at Buffalo.

SUNY Buffalo, as it was called, had a reputable residency program in many specialties, including urology, which I was planning to pursue at the time. After signing a contract with the university's medical school for its urology residency program, I shared this information with my medical colleagues in Chicago, and they approved my choice. They spoke highly of Buffalo's medical program, but they described the city itself as a dull, blue-collar town with cold and prolonged winters. "Not quite the end of the world," as one put it, "but you could almost see it."

On a clear warm morning, near the end of June 1964, I left Chicago with a heavy heart and drove to Buffalo through Canada along the great lakes. I was leaving a city with many good memories I had shared with Judy. The departure was hard on both of us. We had a difficult time saying goodbye. And here I was, yet again terminating a harmonious, happy relationship due to circumstances that appeared to be beyond my control. During this period I was heavily leaning toward going back to Iran. Judy and I promised to stay in touch

The empty highway, still dark, reached the horizon at the hilltops miles ahead. In the opposite direction, a lone truck passed now and then. Patchy clouds over the hilltop changed into rose color, promising a dazzling summer day.

I drove by farming communities, vast orchards, well-groomed vineyards, and undulating hills dotted with grazing farm animals. Away from the hustle and bustle of neighboring towns south of the border, serene isolated villages with clustered houses around church steeples appeared across the landscape.

The serenity, calmness, and isolation of the region lulled me into a reflective mood. I began to wonder about my future. I thought about the pyramid system of the residency program, its rigorous competitiveness and the unpredictability of the outcome as to whether I would be able to finish it and qualify for my chosen specialty.

I knew nothing about the city I was driving to and even less about the hospitals or the people I would be working with. In search of a new life, I felt alone.

All my worldly possessions – a few books and some clothing – barely filled the back seat of my small car.

My thoughts took refuge for temporary relief in the other side of the globe again, back- to the city full of great memories where the sun loomed larger, the sky was a softer blue, and parched mud-walled villages sat among ocher hills and snow-capped mountains.

I had left Iran, but as I heard a compatriot say, Iran had never left me. I was again in the throes of the bipolarity between the two cultures, but as always, such moments left me with conviction of a positive future and an indelible feeling of warmth in the pit of my stomach. I felt confident that the willingness to work hard would help me to overcome any obstacle that life might throw my way.

Why in such reflective moments I invariably arrived on the side of optimism remains a mystery to me. Could deprivation in my past have been a factor for greater appreciation of life? Could a challenging childhood such as mine have given me an optimistic future and the expectation of catching the rainbow throughout my journey? Or would such unhappiness lead to maladjustment and pessimism? Does being the first born with its unconditional and uncontested maternal love have anything to do with it? What about the variables of nurture and culture?

Although our genetic makeup plays an important role in our psyche, my upbringing has also played a significant role in causing me to lean toward optimism.

Unlike the teachings of the West with its heavy emphasis on science and on the Cartesian principle of splitting matter and spirit, the Eastern culture of my earlier years considered divinity and the sanctity of the spirit as integral parts of matter. Persians spoke frequently of god, the divine spirit, harmony, destiny, and love, all in the same interchangeable breath. I have no doubt that I brought this sense of combined body and spirit with me into the medical field, which I'm sure accounts for my ability to succeed in a profession that demands so much of the human soul.

Unlike the west where precedence was given exclusively to the tangible objects, Persians viewed it with a healthy dose of the world beyond. Poetry was at the center of daily life in Persia. People recited poems in conversation, consulted poetry in their relationships, and referenced it in times of uncertainty.

The dominant theme among most popular Persian poets such as Hafez, Molavi, and Khayam with their intoxicating Dionysian love of life was close in philosophy to Sufism. They saw the world as a magical phenomenon that manifested in all aspects of the universe and represented the essence of God. Sufis believe that those with greater spiritual maturity can reach the degree of self-realization necessary for union with this ultimate universal power. In his evolutionary quest of spiritual maturity, they believe that man yearns for unity with God.

Many renowned western scientists reached the same spiritual conclusion. Among them Albert Einstein, who wrote, "The scientists' religious feeling takes the form of rapturous amazement at the harmony of the material law, which, reveals an intelligence of such superiority, that in comparison with it, the highest intelligence of human beings is utterly an insignificant reflection."

The ability to perceive the energy and the divine power present in our interconnected universe is manifested in many forms. Love, goodness, benevolence, the joy of looking at a blade of grass, seeing a world in a drop of water, or eternity in a moment: These all speak of the same belief system. The language is universal and transcends the artificial boundaries of politics and religion.

The positive energy of such a belief system is a powerful source for happy harmonious life and the essence of the Chinese proverb that reminds us, "If you keep a green bough in your heart, the singing birds will come."

Such was the prevalent school of thought intertwined in the collective psyche of the culture that nurtured the first twenty-five years of my life.

Though Sufism was originally a ramification of Islam, the Persians transformed it into a less monolithic and a more humanistic school of thought. The all-inclusive and pantheistic principle of Sufism was the most appealing to Persians and a significant departure from the Islamic principle that believes in Allah as the only God. I had heard that my grandfather was a follower of Sufism, but I never knew much about it when I lived in Iran. It was not until later in the U.S. that I learned the little I know about it now.

These were my reflections as I made my way from Chicago to Buffalo.

The highway and the world appear golden now.

Driving toward Buffalo, as I approach Niagara Falls in this early summer afternoon, I recall the movie called Niagara *I saw with my high school classmate Ali back in Tehran. The movie was a thriller in which Marilyn Monroe and Joseph Cotton played the leading roles in a plot that took place in Niagara Falls. Beside the seductive sauntering of Marilyn Monroe and the beauty of the Falls, I also remember my friend's wistful question: "Do you think it might be possible to visit such a natural beauty someday?" In any other movie, he would have been talking about Marilyn. This time, though, he was talking about the Falls.*

The memory of that scene is still fresh and vibrant as it had been when I was eighteen-years-old; I can't wait to see the Falls, and it doesn't disappoint. I arrive to view its majestic beauty, complete with a picturesque rainbow.

As many times as I have seen it, the drive along the Niagara River leading to the Falls remains as charming as when I experienced it for the first time.

I am uplifted by its natural beauty. Never the same, it varies dramatically according to the season or the time of day.

The wide shimmering blue of the gentle flow begins from Lake Erie, curving and twisting, embracing a couple of small islands on its meandering course before the display of an awe-inspiring finale of the Falls. Here the Falls are flanked by two small towns, one on the American side and the other on the Canadian side, welcoming millions of visitors with colorful gardens and long walking paths along the river. Every nationality can be seen there, every language can be heard among the crowd of visitors strolling on the misty promenade.

After the Falls, the turbulent flow continues to carve through the gorges and canyons searching its destiny eastward. Further down, the river regains its tranquility and flows among the orchards, vineyards, and lush greenery toward the quaint town of Niagara-on-the-Lake, where it joins Lake Ontario.

One version of the genesis of the name Buffalo, the city on its bank, is believed to originate from "Beau Fleuve," or "beautiful river" as the French settlers called it.

There are other versions about the origins of the name of my new city, but this one remains my favorite.

16. CONGRATULATIONS...
UNLESS YOU GO TO JAIL

The two classmates I used to study with during the medical school years, Reza and Parviz, were also in Buffalo, both taking residency in the Ob-Gyn program at the university.

All surgical residents, regardless of their sub-specialties, had to take a year of general surgical rotation. For my rotation, I was assigned to the Buffalo General Hospital.

Buffalo General Hospital was a non-profit private institution providing most of the clinical teaching for the University of Buffalo's medical school. The hospital had a large post-graduate training program in almost all sub-specialties.

I was assigned to a small room with a low bed, two chairs, and a small table in an old two-story building next to the hospital where the house staff lived. The hospital provided uniforms and breakfast. I paid for lunches and dinners from my salary of two hundreds dollar per month.

On-call schedule for surgical residents was generally every third night unless a fellow resident was on vacation or unable to cover. In such cases, we worked every other night.

Routinely we met at 6:00 A.M. in the dining room for breakfast. The on-call resident briefed us on relevant medical events from the night before. The number of residents varied according to the services we covered. Typically the house staff team comprised a chief resident, two to three junior residents, interns, and a few medical students. We began the morning rounds by checking in on all patients scattered throughout the sprawling hospital. The group then dispersed, and each house staff attended his or her specific assignment before joining to assist the assigned attending surgeons in the operating room by 7:30. We met again around 6:00 P.M. for our evening rounds, during which we checked the patients again and then those on call stayed and others finally left.

The heavy workload drained me both mentally and physically. At times it felt like a war of attrition, that the winner would be the last man standing. I drew from inner resources I never knew I had. Motivated at times by anything from adrenalin, professional passion, blind dedication, or simple will power, I kept performing my duties with an uncompromising commitment to the patients in my care.

We spent very long hours on the wards with patients or assisting attending surgeons in the operating room. When on call, the eventful evenings, crowded as they were with emergencies, kept us working through the night.

I ate erratically. Meals were rushed, and lunch became an unaffordable luxury. During long hours of operations, friendly nurses might slip a piece of hard candy under my mask.

Not to be outdone, sleep soon became as much a luxury as food. It was not unusual to be assigned to assist in a long operation the day after a sleepless night. The junior member of the team whose job in assisting was to hold the retractor and observe, learned, as horses do, to sleep while standing up.

The public is under the impression that some degree of machismo is a prerequisite for being a surgeon, that surgeons are not adversely affected by the site of blood or gory scenes. I have seen some medical students who, under the same misconception shied away from the surgical field. Such characteristics are far from reality. I still refuse to see gory movies, nor can I kill an animal or witness it being killed. The site of limb loss in the movies disturbs me, yet I have done many amputations to save lives

The post graduate training program was hierarchical and run heavy-handedly. The department chairmen had total control over the future of the residents. Their recommendations for future positions carried a lot of weight. They decided if and when a resident was ready to leave the training program to begin his surgical career.

During the first year of my assignment in general surgery, I discovered the allure of vascular surgery and began to second-guess my initial leaning toward urology.

I knew as a urologist I would be working more predictable and civilized hours and living a more tranquil life without many emergencies. But that was not enough to draw me away from the excitement and the challenges of vascular surgery, which at the time was at the cutting edge of the surgical world.

In fear of opposition from Dr. W. Staulbitz, the powerful chairman of the Urology Department who was known for his heavy-handed and autocratic approach, I decided to apply for surgical residency programs outside of Buffalo. Few dared to cross swords with Staulbitz. Bailing out of his program would not sit well with him.

When Dr. John Paine, the chairman of the department of surgery, learned about my search for residency outside the area, he called me into his office.

He asked me point-blank: "What is wrong with my program that's making you apply elsewhere?"

"Nothing sir," I replied. "I'd like to stay in Buffalo. I assumed I had no chance of securing a position at U.B., since I had negated my commitment with the urology department."

A man of great integrity, frank and somewhat excitable, he pounded his fist on the desk. "Damn it! If I want a resident in my program, no one is going to dictate to me otherwise. Go ahead and apply to our residency."

So I did.

A few days later, after a meeting of the two chairmen and the medical director of the hospital, Dr. Paine called me back into his office. "Congratulations!" he said. "You are appointed to our residency program, and I expect you to complete it….unless you go to jail."

Considering the program was a pyramid system with many entering and only two reaching the top, it was reassuring to hear from the chairman that I was expected to finish it. But I wondered about the "jail" comment. What did he mean? Did he plan to have me arrested for some crime I didn't even know I had committed? Were doctors in his residency program especially prone to felonies? What potentially wicked road had I just dedicated myself to?

It was not until months later, during the annual social gathering for the residents at Dr. Paine's home that I had a chance to ask him what he meant when he made his cryptic "jail" comment in our meeting. He chuckled, then explained, "I had a resident few years ago from Texas who got involved in a brawl in a bar on Chippewa Street. He got arrested. The police called me up at three o'clock in the morning. I had to go downtown to bail him out. Not an experience I'd care to repeat."

I laughed, relieved, and wished I had asked him about the reference sooner.

Department chairmen played the role of big brother in residents' lives and relationships between residents and faculty tended to be much closer, almost like a family. It made perfect sense. We spent far more time with each other than any of us did with our own families. Not that many of us had families anyway. Very few surgical residents were married; the few who had taken the proverbial plunge walked around either stressed or dazed and hardly seemed the happiest people in the world.

There was no secret about the tough and brutal working hours of a surgical residency. Young surgeons had to pay their dues. The veterans had put in their time. Now they got to sit back a bit and watch us scramble around like jugglers with too many balls in the air.

There were no sympathetic ears for issues such as being burned out, hungry, or tired. Unlike other residents in other specialties who had the opportunity to have a lunch break or leave work at predictable hours, for most of us to have lunch or leave before dark was a luxury we rarely enjoyed. In operating rooms where we spent most of our time, we left when the case was finished and not a second before.

There was zero tolerance for rocking the boat. When a few of us who were chief residents from different departments approached the medical director of the hospital to complain about the laundry service of our uniforms and asked if the uniforms might be cleaned more frequently, he not only rejected such an "absurd request," as he put it, but he informed us that if there were any further meetings between residents for any purpose other than academic interactions, all participants would be fired.

This was hardly a coup d'etat, I thought to myself. *I just wanted some clean clothes to wear.*

But the thought remained unspoken.

As a newcomer I was much more timid and naive about the ways of the hospital and of the country in general. To illustrate the point, I once wrote a letter to the Director General of the IRS to explain about an apparent discrepancy in my tax return.

The letter dated April 14, 1965 read as follows:

Dear Sir:

This is written to explain the $78.50 discrepancy between the sum total $3,974.72 appearing on line five, 1040 A Form.

I am required at the convenience of my employer, The Buffalo General Hospital, to eat my meals on the premises (to ensure twenty-four hour coverage for medical emergencies), and for these meals I am charged $3.00 per week. I have been employed at the hospital for twenty-six weeks and on the advice of the District Director of Internal Service in Buffalo office I have deducted $78.50 from my gross income.

Yours truly.

F. Sadeghian, MD

I never got a letter back, of course. But to this day I laugh at my innocence. After all, who writes a letter to the Director of the IRS informing him about a personal deduction of $78.50 for lunches at work?

In the past couple of decades, there have been major changes of the post-graduate training programs in the United States. Working hours are more civilized, allowing time to attend to the semblance of a normal personal life.

The change was initiated by recommendation of the Bell Commission (1989) in New York and in recognition of the fact that the overworked house staff, whose judgment and performance was being compromised, could and did cause harm to hospital patients. The issue was brought to the fore when a young girl (daughter of a reputable newspaper reporter) was poorly managed in the emergency room of a New York City hospital. Repercussions of the investigative pursuit of this incident led to the formation of the Bell Commission and New York State Code 405 with new guidelines approved by the state legislatures with the hope of preventing similar incidents.

The guidelines recommended by the Bell commission were more or less followed in most specialties. But some, especially among the surgeons, could not rigidly adhere to the commission's mandates. Unpredictable hours and an overwhelming workload for the surgeons necessitated only partial compliance with the new code. Since in the real world it is not unusual for a surgeon to be up with an emergency during the night and expected to cope with a full schedule the following day, how some argued, could doctors deal with such demanding hours of a surgical practice without the rigorous and grueling training to prepare them for it?

To combat fatigue, most surgeons learned to take a nap in any position or location. I have witnessed the remarkable ability of some surgical colleagues to take a cat nap in the middle of a conversation! A short cat nap to most, and to me still, is extremely refreshing, no mater how brief.

Medical conferences became prime sleeping time. The lights would dim. The medical slides would be projected onto the white screen. Heads would nod, and snores would start.

I remember covering the emergency room on an especially busy night. I had just gone to bed when the telephone rang and an irritated nurse wanted to know if I was going to come in to see a particular patient. Irritated, I began to chastise the nurse over the phone.

"Didn't I see this patient already?" I insisted. "Didn't I write orders for his admission?"

She informed me that none of that had happened, and I realized, to my profound embarrassment, that I hadn't seen the patient at all. I'd only dreamed I had! I apologized to the nurse, hung up the phone, and crawled out of bed for another grueling, sleepless, and unrelenting full day of work.

Eventually, the near normal life during the four months of rotation in pathology provided me with an opportunity to play tennis again. I had not touched a tennis racquet since I had played on the grass courts of the Old Church hospital in London.

In Buffalo, I played tennis with Takita, a Japanese resident in the cardio-thoracic program. Taki as we called him, was a few years older than I and had married a French girl in the residency program in psychiatry. I saw a great deal of Taki and Claire during our residency and for many years after when they stayed in the area and practiced their respective specialties. Back then, we played on the hospital's single asphalt tennis court during lunch hours while keeping our ears tuned to the telephone installed next to the court. The court's surface was in bad shape with major cracks and faded boundary lines. I decided to contact the administration and ask if they might consider resurfacing the court or at the very least, re-lining it. They did. They took down the net, put in evenly spaced lines, and turned our tennis court into a parking lot.

Buffalo General Hospital had one of the better residency programs in internal medicine and attracted bright graduates from the top medical schools in the country. The chairman of the department was a bright and dynamic physician who, like many others in his position, did not shy away from any opportunity to be under the lime light.

Every department held weekly mortality and morbidity conferences known as "M & M," which were considered an important part of teaching programs during which the disease, its course, treatments, and finally the pathology or autopsy findings, if any, were discussed. The formats of such meetings were predictable, and the ensuing debates and criticism were often earnest and instructive.

I was asked during my rotation in pathology to attend the medical M & M meeting in order to report the autopsy findings of a patient.

The conference began first thing in the morning in the main dining room over a skimpy breakfast. I found myself alone at a table when the chairman of the department of medicine eased into the seat next to mine.

Leaning over, he asked, "Why are you at this meeting?"

I informed him, "I'm presenting the post-mortem findings and pathological diagnosis."

He said, "I see" and proceeded to ask me a long series of questions regarding my diagnosis as we waited for the meeting to begin.

The room filled quickly with attending and residents and medical students. The senior attending, Dr. Ramsdel Gurney, the physician under whose care the patient had been treated, began his presentation. He touched on the onset of the illness, its prolonged course, and the various investigative steps and treatments that his team had pursued. A lengthy interactive discussion followed. Everyone seemed to be puzzled by the complexity of the case, and wild guesses and gross misdiagnoses abounded. At last the chairman spoke, and without blinking an eye offered his probable diagnosis, exactly as I had informed him at our table a few minutes earlier. When I presented the post-mortem findings confirming the chairman's diagnosis, all seemed awed by his wisdom and clinical acuity. I thought that he guessed it right due to the information I gave him, simply because the others were so far off the mark.

I could have been wrong in my assumption, but showmanship and self-promotion prevailed in the competitive academic atmosphere. Most of the academic papers were not entirely original and did not always contribute to the advancement of medicine. To be tenured required publishing papers, the quality of which was often not the highest priority. I found this practice to be one of the more intellectually dishonest and troubling aspects of academic medicine.

Some of the best-intentioned research was biased in favor of the view of whomever supported the studies, and almost all studies were supported by the drug companies or by the medical industrial complex.

The influence of drug companies began early during the years of the medical school. The drug representatives regularly brought lunches to the meetings for the young doctors in training or for the medical students in the teaching hospital. Later, as we moved up the ladder of seniority, these young doctors and medical students were invited to dinners, golf outings, or company-sponsored trips with conferences focusing on the efficacy of that company's products. This grooming by the medical industrial complex was so pervasive that no one seemed to be bothered by it or compelled to question the motives of the sponsors. The sponsors' modus operandi seemed parallel to the lobbying of special interest groups on Capitol Hill, making the whole affair appear legitimate and part of the fabric of democracy. I found this trend disturbing and did my best to avoid meeting with the representatives of drug companies. It would be unfair to paint all with the same brush; there were some who marched to a different drummer.

It would be also unfair if I did not add my admiration and respect for the chairman of the department of medicine as I began to know him years later through closer professional contacts. During this time as a member of the same practicing group of physicians and having had ample opportunity to observe his approach to some of our mutual patients, I was impressed by his devotion and genuine care, which put more doubt in my original assumption of the M & M incident. He put the University of Buffalo's medical school on the map and trained many who became the bright stars in both the research and clinical fields of medicine in the country.

The autocratic hierarchy of the surgical residency was more severe in certain programs. It was well known in the surgical community that some tyrannical chairmen treated their residents more like children, slapping their hands with surgical instruments during surgery if they made a wrong move or asking them to stand in the corner of the operating room.

Unfortunately, some of these tyrants lurked among the surgical faculty at Children's Hospital. With no professionalism to speak of and with little rapport between faculty and residents, we were treated poorly and used as virtual slaves for cheap labor. On call every other night, as we were, our wages during this rotation came to about twenty-five cents an hour, obviously well below the minimum wage in the 1960s. Not that even a high hourly wage could have justified some of the mental and verbal abuse perpetuated by several of the higher ranking doctors.

It was sad to see how surgical residency programs transformed so many young, idealistic, and multi-faceted candidates into one-dimensional automatons as their end product. Consequently, the surgical community seemed to have more than its share of the socially inept, insulated individuals who were detached from their surroundings and totally absorbed in the heavy demand of their profession. While some former physicians have become highly-regarded poets, writers, musicians, and painters, it is noteworthy that none manifested that artistic side when fully immersed in the practice of his or her profession.

Contrary to public assumption, all surgeons are not created equal. Some were outstanding, most were adequate, and a few were incompetent bordering on becoming a danger to public.

The standard of surgical practice at the BGH was as good as any teaching center in the country, but we also had our share of mediocre surgeons.

On a rotational basis, we were assigned to all three divisions with the responsibility of caring for the patients of the attendings within the division.

My first assignment was in Division One.

The chief of this division was a small man with a gaunt face, well-groomed curly hair, polished fingernails, and seemingly friendly eyes. Politically powerful, he had built a surgical empire not because of his ability as an exceptional surgeon but due to his showmanship and good business sense.

The Chief, insisted on making rounds with an entourage of doctors that included his sidekick, and a group of residents, interns, and an assortment of medical students. Most of time he had no idea about the medical conditions of the patients, and it was our responsibility to give him pertinent information before entering a patient's room. He'd use the information to make a patients believe he knew more about them than he really did.

He didn't spend much time in the operating room. On rare occasions, when he did, he was assisted every step of the way by his associate. Soon however, he would leave the operating room and leave his associate to complete the crucial part of the operation, in order to report to the referring physicians the success of surgery, and the operative findings. He took pride and emphasized the importance of proper communication with the referring physicians. One could learn how to build a successful medical empire, as he had, by observing his modus operandi.

To them, speed in performing surgery was important since they had a huge load to handle. Their promotional skill and the political power among the referring physicians made their practice thrive.

His sidekick was a hard-working surgeon who had a friendly smile and sincerely believed in the service he provided for his patients. Working with him as most of us did during the rotation was a different experience. In his mid-forties, he was an excitable man with a ruddy complexion, a protruding chin, and a big nose. His enthusiasm for his work led him to boast about and exaggerate the number of operations he had performed or the successes he had achieved in treating different surgical conditions. He walked fast, talked faster, and never opened a door as most do by the handle. Instead he'd push the door with his shoulder as if still tackling for his high school football team. If during an operation, he stuck his assistant with a needle or a sharp instrument as he often did in his haste, he expected no reaction. Putting his rough edges aside, he was dedicated and caring.

One night when I was on call as senior resident, a patient was brought in from Attica prison diagnosed with a ruptured abdominal aneurysm. It was rather unusual for a private hospital to receive patients from the prison population since such patients were typically treated at the Erie County Medical Center.

The patient was admitted under the care of a vascular surgeon who no longer did major vascular surgery and had limited his practice to patients with venous disease. He had a huge following of patients with varicosities and related problems, which he treated with injections of sclerosing solution whether they needed it or not. (Such solutions obliterate the veins by scar tissue.)

The surgeon was an introvert, stone deaf, who hardly spoke with anyone and seemed to live in his own world. He had a plethoric face with thick eyebrows and a prominent nose with a large black mole next to it. He insisted on wearing old shrunken suits, which bulged over his fat stomach. He was a gentle, devoted soul who drank perhaps more than his share and who took care of his polio-stricken wife for years while she lived on an iron lung. He liked hunting and collected guns and tragically committed suicide with one of them in the 1980s.

After I worked up the prison-patient, I called him to report my diagnosis and the need for urgent surgery. He showed up looking even more turgid than usual. I could tell he'd had his share of drink for the evening. Recognizing his limitations, he played second fiddle in the operating room, helping me to repair the ruptured abdominal aneurysm. During surgery, I learned that the patient was some kind of a folk hero, a notorious bank robber named Willie Sutton who everybody but me seemed to know about. I learned that Sutton was also an escape artist who had managed to slip out of some of the toughest prisons with the highest security. Most knew of Willie Sutton's congressional hearing and his famous response when asked, "Why do you rob banks?" He had answered "Because that's where the money is."

Willie did well and pulled through the life-threatening disease and its fifty percent mortality rate. He stayed in intensive care for several days during which this frail old man (he must have been in his late sixties) who was tied to all kinds of tubes, monitors, and a respirator, was watched around the clock by two armed security guards. He soon recovered, and we sent him back to Attica prison.

The chief of Division Two, was a knowledgeable and dedicated man who had a tic that during the earlier weeks of my rotation, I mistook for a smile, and not knowing how to respond, I too returned with a smile.

His bow tie, round glasses, trim athletic physique, and overall mannerism spoke of elite schooling, and he seemed to be intolerant of anyone with anything less. Most of his patients were among Buffalo's affluent blue-bloods. The chief's father had been a well known surgeon in Buffalo, and his children and grandchildren all became physicians. During earlier rotations in his service as a junior resident, I was a nonentity to him. Later during my senior year, however, he warmed considerably to the point that, with him assisting me, I performed most of his operations, a privilege very few shared.

Once his initial aura of superiority melted away, one could see a decent, hard-working man with much dedication toward his patients and great pride in his profession.

The chief of division three had been at one time among the bright stars in the surgical universe and had pioneered cardiac surgery in Buffalo. No longer active in cardiac surgery since the appointment of a younger and gifted Hungarian surgeon as the chief of cardiac surgery, he had confined his practice to general and thoracic surgery instead. He was a man of considerable wisdom and excellent judgment who was capable of setting aside his ego for the sake of his patients.

I discovered this admirable trait when I was chief resident and had taken one week vacation to stay home with our new born son..

He called in the middle of night. Apologetic, he said, "Fero, I know you are off this week, but I just admitted my good friend Dr. G. with an acute abdomen. Could you come in and give me a hand?"

Acute abdomen represents some sort of catastrophe in the belly, the nature of which could range from a simple ruptured appendix to a variety of other serious causes. Such an illness could present the surgeon with a variety of unpredictable challenges, especially in older patients like Dr. G. who was also a highly respected orthopedic surgeon in the community.

I told him "I'll be there" and shortly after, arrived at the hospital to give him a hand.

I was pleased to help. It was a feather in my cap to be asked. (After all, I too was a surgeon and not immune to having a sizable ego.) This simple gesture of setting aside ego to ask for help elevated him in my eyes. As it turned out the problem was much simpler than either of us had anticipated.

A few years later the same orthopedic surgeon who was then a consultant for the navy in Washington, approached me with the idea of joining Walter Reed Hospital where there was a need for a vascular surgeon. I was settling in Buffalo by then and decided to stay.

To be a patient's advocate, which I believe is the prime responsibility of a physician, demands the kind of humility I witnessed from him. But there were others with huge egos, self-serving interests, and very little regard for the welfare of their patients. I saw this unfortunate scenario play out during my rotation at the Veterans Administration Hospital.

VA Hospitals were known to have less rigorous supervision of the residents than other teaching hospitals such as Buffalo Buffalo General where the supervising faculty breathed down our necks.

During my three-month rotation at the VA Hospital in 1967, I was assigned to help the chief resident to operate on an elderly patient with a blockage of the bile passage. Such blockages are commonly caused by gall stones or tumors. In this case, because of the patient's age, a tumor seemed the more likely culprit. Under the presumptive diagnosis of a tumor of the head of the pancreas, the chief resident was ready to go ahead with an operation known as the "Whipple Procedure," which was specifically designed for this problem.

This surgery was among the more extensive and challenging operations that a surgeon could perform. It not only required removal of the deeply-seated pancreas, but also of the duodenum, part of the stomach, the biliary duct, and the rearrangement of the continuity of the gastro-intestinal track. The operation carried a significant mortality and morbidity rate, especially in the hands of an inexperienced surgeon. The surgery for removal of the stone, on the other hand, was much more simple and much less traumatizing to the patient and carried far fewer complications.

Needless to say, that differentiation between the two at the time of surgery was the most important judgment call on the part of the surgeon. And in order to identify the exact underlying cause of blockage, there were well established surgical guidelines the surgeon needed to follow in order to come to the right conclusion. (This was before the development and use of more precise diagnostics tools like CT Scans and MRIs.) Without taking the prerequisite steps, Dr. C., eager to perform his first Whipple Procedure, had already concluded that the patient's cause of blockage was a tumor, and he was ready to go ahead with the more radical surgery.

I suggested to him the need for further surgical evaluation including an X-ray of the common duct to ascertain whether his presumptive diagnosis was correct. Already determined and with his ego hurt, he refused to hear me and began the initial steps toward radical operation.

I was in a bind. How could I assist an act that could possibly harm the patient? Admittedly, I wanted eagerly and under the correct circumstance to be the first assistant in such an exciting operation.

I was aware that the hierarchy and pecking order were not unlike the military chain of command with its requirement of complete obedience and submission to the judgment calls of superiors. I decided to bear the consequences of insubordination, whatever they may be, and informed him that I could not continue to assist him. I suggested getting another resident to help him, and after my replacement arrived, I took my gloves off and left the operating room.

The incident was reported to the chief of surgery who arrived immediately and concurred that further steps were necessary to establish the definitive diagnosis. Subsequently it was proved that the blockage was indeed caused by a stone and not by a tumor. Lesser surgery was performed. No one ever said anything to me about the incident. No one criticized me or thanked me for it. I wasn't looking for praise or recognition, though. I was just happy I had made the right call.

Pt. IV – Nancy

17. VEILED, CAPTIVATING EYES

I'd been in Buffalo for only a few weeks. I barely knew my surroundings and wasn't yet familiar with the sprawling corridors of the hospital. I was assigned to assist Dr. B. to repair a hernia in operating room number five. That is where I met Nancy for the first time

Ready to assist Dr. B., I noticed my mask had slipped upward, and was obstructing my view. I asked the facilitating nurse, known as the "circulator," if she could adjust the mask for me. Although this type of simple request happened every day, the nurse simply stared at me and didn't move. The nursing instructor, standing in the corner of the operating room in her supervisory role, informed me that the quiet nurse was a student assigned to the operating room for the first time. So I asked the student nurse again. This time louder.

Like others, her head and face were almost completely covered by a cap and mask. Although tall, in her formless baggy blue operating-room gown, she remained indistinguishable from the others. She might as well have been wearing a burka. But when she came closer, she stunned me with the most unusual and radiant eyes. They bore an Asiatic slant, with a lovely shade of bluish green, easy to recall but impossible to define. Their warmth drew me in instantly, and I felt an urgency to know more about this mystery woman.

I saw those captivating eyes again a few days later in the small smoke-filled coffee shop where the house staff and nurses gathered. Now the mysterious woman wore blue jeans and a short-sleeved cotton blouse. She had her hair parted in the middle with a long braid tied off with a red ribbon on either side. Our eyes met, and we silently acknowledged the mutual curiosity of our previous half-masked glance.

A few nights later, while working the evening shift, I saw her again, this time in the medical ward where I had stopped off to see a patient. I approached her.

"You adjusted my mask the other day in the operating room," I said. An opening line only a surgeon could use.

"Yes," she replied. "It was embarrassing. I didn't know what you were asking me to do."

She was looking at my name embroidered in bold on my uniform as she spoke.

I had been in the U.S. long enough to know the difficulty people had in pronouncing my name.

Do you know how to pronounce my name?" I asked

She said, "Yes" and proceeded to pronounce it perfectly.

Nancy was twenty-one and would be graduating from nursing school in a few months.

We had our first date in a restaurant in Williamsville. She wore a loose-fitting blouse and a jean skirt. I wore a suit and tie. She wore her hair Jacquelyn Kennedy style. With those lovely slanted green-blue eyes and her tall, slender figure, she looked like a model or a movie star.

I complimented her on her dress.

"I made it myself," she said.

"Really?"

"Sure. I make all my clothing."

That impressed me. Frankly, I had trouble doing my own laundry. The thought of making my own clothes made open-heart surgery seem simple by comparison.

Nancy spoke freely of her family, and I listened with genuine interest.

She struck me as fiercely self-reliant. She loved work and family equally and accepted hardships as a part of life. Poised and graceful, she came across as needing nothing in her world that might distract her from her simple love of life. Sitting there at our first date, I already felt myself being drawn in, seduced in a way I'd never experienced before. Without knowing why, I knew I would need to see Nancy again.

On our second date, I told Nancy that in Persia, I had four wives and nine children. She gave me the same blank stare she'd given me in the operating room. Although polygamy was one of the few facts she knew about the Persian culture, she did not believe me and finally realized I was joking. We both laughed and promised we'd continued to see each other.

Still uncertain at this juncture about my future plans, which encompassed a multitude of possibilities, I was not quite ready to commit myself to a long-term relationship.

One major issue was the uncertainty of where I wanted to settle. I contemplated returning to the old country, and as Nancy and I grew closer, I spoke about the possibility of the two of us living in Iran. She said she would live in Iran if we had to. Though I knew she could not possibly have a realistic image of life in Iran, I felt confident that if any American woman could live there, she would be the one. Her resourcefulness, frugality, self-sufficiency, and willingness to accept hardships made her adaptable and impressively strong.

I told her that if I ever decided to marry in the United States, she would be the one. We remained friends but went our separate ways for the time being.

I moved out of the resident's dorm and rented a furnished apartment on Symphony Circle.

Shortly after settling in, Nas informed me that he, Barbara, and their six-month-old daughter Kim would like to stay with me on their way from Chicago to England where Nas had taken a fellowship position with John Charnley, the renowned pioneer in joint replacement. I was looking forward to seeing Nas and his family and spending time with them. As it turned out, I was bombarded with emergencies and could not leave the operating room for even a short visit.

I had left the key to my one-bedroom apartment in the mail box and, unable to find time for shopping, left them with no food. Their stay was brief. They improvised a bed for Kim in an empty drawer of my dresser and, finding one rotten onion as the refrigerator's sole inhabitant, they left the following day after calling me in the hospital to say goodbye. I apologized to Nas who just laughed and said, "We had to go. I'm sorry we couldn't stay longer. Just go get yourself some food before you starve to death!"

Soon after, I moved again, this time into a quaint attic apartment which I shared with fellow resident Alberto, on the third floor of an older home on Norwood Avenue. The charming street spoke of the city's better days with its majestic trees and a variety of spacious, older homes.

Buffalo had started to close in on me; I had difficulty adjusting to the industrial blue-colored town that held little excitement for an energetic bachelor. I was nostalgic for a more vibrant life in a more cosmopolitan town.

I never thought I would stay an extra day in Buffalo beyond the required time of my training. I considered the area as my temporary home. I never even bothered to learn most of the street names.

"Why bother?" I thought. "I will be leaving this town in four to five years."

For a diversion in Buffalo, most residents went to the now-famous Anchor Bar around the corner. The establishment was owned by Theresa and Frank, a married couple in their fifties. Their famous chicken wings dipped in a special hot sauce later became known as "Buffalo wings" (although no one in Buffalo calls them that) and put the city on the map of culinary fast food around the country.

Through the Buffalo International Institute I met and got acquainted with a few families and attended parties among the upper crust of Buffalo society.

I met the renowned Budapest Quartet at the home of the University of Buffalo's distinguished English professor, Oscar Silverman. I had the pleasure and privilege of meeting Bishop Scaif and had dinner with his family on a couple of occasions at his mansion on Lincoln Parkway where he lived with his wife and two daughters with all the elegance and decorum of the old aristocracy. He was a Renaissance-man, brimming with intellectual vigor and an interest in all things spiritual and artistic. At the Snow Ball of 1965, which I attended as their guest, I remember him being among the last to leave the dance floor.

The annual Snow Ball was sponsored by the junior board of Buffalo General Hospital and was held in the large ballroom of the old Statler Hotel in honor of the debutantes of Buffalo's high society. The Snow Ball holds a special place in my heart: It's where I knew for the first time that I was ready to settle down.

Nancy graduated from nursing school and was recently promoted as head nurse of a medical unit. I saw her almost daily during my rounds. Though we had not dated for almost a year, she had never left my mind, and we both knew that we were watching each other from a distance.

I was thirty-one years old and would complete my residency in less than two years. I wanted to have a family. I wanted to be rooted.

I felt Nancy possessed the qualities I looked for in a wife. When I asked her if she wanted to be my partner in life and marry me, her response, in her quiet and reserved way, was an overwhelming yes.

At the Snow Ball of 1965, we announced our engagement. Tall and slim in her elegant beaded white gown, Nancy looked stunning, and those unusually beautiful eyes radiated more than ever with pure pleasure and absolute joy.

Shortly before announcing our engagement, I met Nancy's mother in a duplex apartment among a row of similar buildings closely constructed to each other. She lived on the upper floor with her son John who at the time was away serving in Germany.

A high-strung, hard working attractive woman, Nancy's mother worked as a secretary and had lived alone after the death of Nancy's father a few years earlier.

Nancy's mother coming from a generation who had been through depression and war, seemed to be obsessively preoccupied with trivial monetary affairs and overly concerned about financial security. Adding to it the cultural provincialism, I knew that we lived in a different world.

Recognition of this fact and concern that to some degree this may have influenced Nancy did not phase me. The ability to change my own life led me to assume that I could change others, especially those near and dear to me. And in reflective moments of examining my own life, it became clear that in the context of my favorite motto, the Serenity Prayer:

"Lord grant me the serenity to accept the things that I cannot change, the courage to change the things that I can, and the wisdom to know the difference."

I have frequently overestimated my ability to change others.

On January 28, 1966, on a frigid and snowy Buffalo day, Nancy and I were married in her neighborhood church. Unable to take more than couple days off, we spent forty-eight hours in Toronto and returned to Buffalo to work. We promised to take our honeymoon that summer as we did, in Prince Edward Island, Canada.

We settled into my third floor apartment. The depleted refrigerator and sparse kitchen from my bachelor days surrendered to a new wave of aromas. The cold apartment grew warm. We celebrated our first Christmas together and bought our first tree.

To acquire our tree, we took an entire day off just to ride out into the countryside. A thick but soft layer of snow covered the roads and the fields, and glittering ice hung from the evergreen trees like crystal from a chandelier. We found a small lot just off the main road where a man and his daughter sold Christmas trees newly cut from the large parcel of land they owned. Nancy spotted "the perfect tree" and gleefully led me over to it. We brushed the snow from its surface, and I agreed: The tree was indeed perfect.

"Tall and beautiful," I said to Nancy. "Just like you."

She laughed and said, "Pay the man." So I did, and he helped us carry the tree out and slide it onto the ski rack on top of my white Corvair.

When we got home, we lugged the tree up the three flights of stairs to our apartment. Nancy decorated the tree with the care and attention one might use to dress a child. We loved our new tree's soft green needles and the fragrance of its freshly cut stump so much that we kept it for over two months after Christmas. By the time we finally agreed to give it up, it had become so dried out that by dragging it through the apartment to discard it, the tree was stripped completely bare and left behind thousands of prickly needles, which we had to pick up by hand one-by-one for days after.

Our limited income provided for the bare essentials and very little else. For entertainment we drove along the Niagara River to the Falls and sometimes beyond to Niagara-on-the-Lake for a drink in Oban Inn by the cozy fireplace of its charming pub.

In the middle of our first married summer under the hot roof of our attic apartment, a distant relative called from Cleveland saying he wanted to visit us on the way to Niagara Falls. I sensed uneasiness and apprehension in Nancy. For me, growing up as I had, nothing could be more normal than having family and other guests over for lunch or dinner. For Nancy, however, guests, especially unexpected ones, meant stress and a confusing break in her routine. In Iranian culture, personal freedoms may be more limited in many ways, but greater emphasis on social communality gives a freer flow to social situations. In America, guests are welcomed; in Iran, they are sacred.

My cousin Khosro, whose family lived in the same home with us during the last year of my high school and early medical school years in Tehran, was now studying at Case Western University in Cleveland three hours away by car. He had recently married a charming, multilingual Argentinean-raised classmate, originally from Lithuania whose family had immigrated to the U.S.

We saw Khosro and Nerhinga during the weekends, either in Cleveland or in Buffalo. In Cleveland, they took us to a number of concerts led by famed conductor George Szell, and we reciprocated by taking them to our beautiful (and acoustically superior) concert hall in Buffalo.

Nancy was in her final days of pregnancy and already three weeks late when she called me while I was in the middle of a complicated surgery in the operating room at Buffalo General.

One of the nurses answered.

"Dr. Sadeghian," she said, "your wife is on the phone."

I wrapped a sterile towel around my gloved hand and approached the phone while the nurse held the receiver to my ear.

"Fero," Nancy shouted, "I am having contractions! I think they are real!"

There was no way I could leave the operating room.

Excited, happy, and frustrated not to be able able to leave, I tried to conceal my emotions as I completed the operation.

With the help of operating room staff, we contacted an ob-gyn colleague who drove to our apartment and brought Nancy to the maternity ward four floors above where I was working and where I joined her just minutes before our first son Scott was born.

Taking on the roles of full time mother and housewife, Nancy stopped working.

As much as we liked our quaint attic apartment, with our new addition, we needed a new home. Soon we found a furnished home in the modest and quiet neighborhood of Kenmore, a well-kept Buffalo suburb, and rented it from a university professor who was going on sabbatical overseas for one year.

I would be graduating in July of 1968, only a few months away. The U.S. was at the height of the Vietnam War. I was certain with my specialty in surgery being in high demand, I would be drafted for the war. The last year's graduates of our program were all drafted.

With my love of flying and the impression that such opportunity was more readily available in the Navy or Air force, I decided to volunteer. But when I contacted the recruiting center, I was told since the army did not have enough doctors, especially surgeons, all medical personnel had to enter a pool from which different branches of the armed forces drew their quota. I went for my physical examination and received an A-1 status. Shortly after, I received orders from army headquarters in Maryland instructing me to be ready to leave for training camp in a few weeks.

But that was the last communication I ever received from the armed forces. American involvement in Vietnam had begun to abate, and I guess the government forgot about me.

Thirty years later, when some of the truth behind the political motives and conduct in the war came to light, I felt fortunate not to have been part of it.

I was finally ready to cut the umbilical cord from the educational institutions. I was thirty-three years old.

Since I had no license to practice medicine in New York, I took a position as cancer research surgeon at Roswell Park Memorial Institute where I focused primarily on breast cancer.

Along the way, I applied for the notoriously difficult New York State medical license which included some of the basic science courses.

I set aside a few hours every day to study while working at Roswell and was happy to pass the grueling three-day written exam that allowed me to practice medicine. Not very many sat for this exam. The few who did were mostly foreign graduates who planned to stay around the area.

An article appeared in one of the two Buffalo's major daily news paper shortly after the results of the medical exam was published. The columnist alluded to the "strange sounding names," mine among them, of the individuals who had passed the test. With typical xenophobic prejudice, the writer lamented the loss of the "Irish and European sounding names of the past." Reading such a brazenly prejudiced view in the column of the major newspaper of the town further confirmed the parochialism of the Buffalo community. Ironically, those individuals with strange names, some scientists, others teachers and clinicians, contributed significantly to the Buffalo medical community. Among them, an Indian pediatric surgeon who put Buffalo on the map as a center of excellence for pediatric cardiac surgery. There was also a Japanese surgeon whose cancer research became well-respected in the international scientific community.

Buffalo was a blue collar industrial town and depended heavily on steel-mills for its economy and cultural identity. The city remained isolated in many ways from the larger American community. Buffalo had once been an economic powerhouse with enormous wealth surging along with the flow of the Niagara River and its newfound ability to produce mass amounts of electricity. Steady economic decline, however, left the city in bad shape while a few old wealthy and influential families jealously guarded the exhausted glory of its past.

The provincialism and isolationism that imbued Western New York seemed more pronounced than in the rest of the country. I was surprised how uninformed average Americans were about the rest of the world. Even among the better educated, the knowledge about other cultures was pathetically lacking. The issue seemed irrelevant to most Americans. There was no need for them to know much about the world beyond the security of their own borders. In contrast, the third world nations had a keen awareness and interest of the world beyond their own.

Lack of information about a foreign land such as Iran, was the cause of questions like "Have you ever seen snow?" "Did you use utensils for food?" "Have you ever eaten chicken?" "Did you ride a lot of camels?" and many other misconceived questions along those lines. There was a vague romantic notion about Persia and a total confusion with the country's new name of "Iran."

The more informed identified Iran with the Shah, Sorya, oil, carpets, and cats.

As disappointed as I was about the discouraging and prejudiced tone of the newspaper's comments, I was also well aware of the fact that no other nation on earth welcomed new immigrants as warmly and genuinely as did the United State of America.

Some prejudice notwithstanding, the Buffalo community had its many wonderful inherent qualities. The hardworking German, Polish, and Italian immigrants were decent folks who cared deeply about their community and gave the city the reputation of being the "City of Good Neighbors." The city's rich history had sprinkled Buffalo with beautiful buildings and architectural gems. The city had exceptional parks and majestic streets with landscaping rarely seen in other cities. Its suburbs offered a tranquil life with easy access to downtown and to the large public university. The summers were as good as anywhere in the world. Even the harsh prolonged winters with significant snow accumulation offered some of the most beautiful winter wonders imaginable.

When viewed under a microscope, snowflakes are a marvel of so many varieties of design. Each region according to the experts has its own unique design easily distinguishable from others. According to one expert I heard, the microscopic view of snow flakes of the Lake Erie region are among the most beautifully designed. Although I cannot be the judge of the microscopic beauty of its snowflakes, the cumulative impact of such flakes during Buffalo's frequent snow storms was and remains a truly lovely sight.

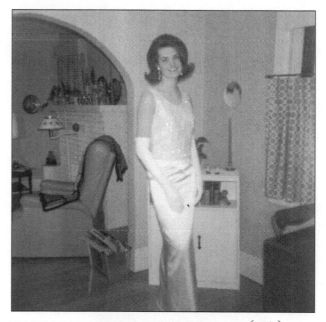

NANCY BEFORE ATTENDING THE SNOW BALL (1965)

NANCY AND I (1970)

18. A BALANCED LIFE

In 1968, Nancy gave birth to our second child, a beautiful girl we named Tracy. My mother arrived from Iran soon after to stay with us for a few months.

My uncle arranged the trip for her. She came to U.S. as the sole passenger on one of those humongous military transport planes with a cargo hold the size of a football field.

She had mentioned to me her intention to come to the U.S. to see our new born daughter Tracy, but I had no idea about the mode of her transport or to the timing of her arrival.

I had just sat for dinner when the telephone rang.

"Fraydoon!" shouting happily as she always was speaking with me.

Excited to hear her voice, I shouted back, "Salaam Madar! Where are you?"

"I am at the airport."

"That is great! How was your flight?"

"Very comfortable," she said. "The crews were wonderful and took good care of me. I had the whole plane to myself to sleep and do my praying."

Confused, wondering what airline allowed her to occupy the plane by herself, I asked her, "What airline did you fly?"

"I came in an empty military plane," she said as if it were the most normal thing in the world.

"Which airport are you at Mother?"

"I don't know. The pilot is here. I will give him the phone."

"Dr. Sadeghian," a man said in Farsi, "We are at LaGuardia and Khanoom is fine."

"Well, I will leave right now, but it will take me at least eight hours to get there."

"Yes of course. That is fine," he said. "We will make proper arrangements for Khanoom's stay until you arrive."

"Very good. Could you put my mother on?"

He did, and I told my mother I'd be there as soon as possible and briefly explained the distance involved.

She sounded surprised to learn about the drive being such a long distance. Visitors to the U.S. are often surprised at how vast the country is. In many parts of the world, an eight-hour drive can get you from one end of the country to the other. In the U.S. it barely gets you across New York State.

This was the first of many trips my mother took every few years in order to visit us. She was a delight to have around, and Nancy got along with her quite well. She was bit of a puzzle to our kids, though. They could not understand her praying five times per day. All of her standing, kneeling, bending, and a lot of whispering to no one in particular confused them. They often interrupted her prayers by trying to climb on her back for piggyback rides when she bent down to place her forehead against the piece of clay, which symbolically represented the house of God.

In 1969 Nancy was pregnant for the third time and was due in a few months. Our rented two bedroom apartment was already crowded for our family of four. With the new arrival due in a few months and with my mother's visit, we badly needed a larger home.

Nancy and I talked about buying a house. She wanted a colonial home in the southern suburb of the city.

Knowing Nancy's deliberate and time-consuming decision-making process, even in trivial matters, I knew that the chances of finding her ideal home in a short period of time were next to zero. So when a colleague mentioned a house for sale across from his in a very nice neighborhood, I decided to check it out.

The house was a charming ranch with three bedrooms located on a street occupied by young families with small children and easy access to the hospital. I bought it.

When I told Nancy, she cried.

Still, she understood that this home was an interim home and was purchased in order to accommodate our rapidly expanding family. I promised her that I would continue to look for her "dream home."

To mortgage it, I spoke with a patient of mine in the banking business who asked me about the make up of the home. Although I had supervised the construction of my parent's home in Tehran, I had no idea about the material or quality of the homes in this country, and all I could tell him about the house was it was white!

Nancy looked more pregnant than usual. I asked her obstetrician if she was carrying more than one. "What do you know about pregnancy?" he said. "You are a surgeon."

A few weeks after moving to our new home, Nancy gave birth to twins.

The house turned out to be a perfect interim home for us. We had little furniture, but we were wall to wall in high chairs, cribs, toys and babies. We now had four children under two and half years old.

I admired Nancy for her efficiency, resourcefulness, and dedication during the upbringing of our children. I was of little help and as busy as I was, I felt her responsibilities were no less than mine.

I left very early in the morning and came home after dark. My plate was full. Having just passed the New York State medical board, I was now preoccupied with the logistics of starting a surgical practice and preparing to take my surgical boards.

Certification by the American Board of Surgery is another important hurdle for a surgeon to overcome. The surgical board gives the official seal of the approval of a surgeon as being qualified to perform his or her duties. The exam was given in two parts: written and oral. The former had a failure rate of nearly fifty percent and the latter around thirty percent.

By this time going back to the old country especially with my eligibility for military draft in Iran and the culture shock for my young family was no longer an option. Though Nancy never expressed opposition to going back to Iran, she was clearly relieved once we decided to stay and settle in the United States for good.

I became a U.S. citizen shortly after and accepted the fact that I would be staying in Buffalo perhaps a little longer, but I still stubbornly refused to remember the names of the streets.

The two years we lived in our Williamsville home revolved mostly around our children.

High-chairs around the dinner table, Nancy spoon-feeding children in turn, and by the time the last one was fed, the first was hungry again. The busy backyard with screams and laughers of Scott, Tracy, and the twins, Mark and Todd, the screeching of the swing set, the faces smeared with chocolate ice cream, chasing and splashing each other with the water hose, the occasional cry of one consoled by the other. These are among my most vivid memories of the two years we lived at our house in Williamsville.

I loved my profession and knew from the beginning that the clinical aspect of surgery and patient care was what I valued most. I considered a surgical career as the most rewarding, allowing me to help patients in overcoming the pain and misery of disease. The scientific research and the academic part of my profession did not interest me. I could never envision myself spending hours in a lab or researching a scientific paper in the library. I did not have the scientific mind or the desire to immerse myself in the lab. I was always fascinated by the bigger picture and had a tendency to gloss over details except when I dealt with clinical situations. I also found climbing the ladder in the academic world with all its back-scratching and political maneuvering, or gathering power through building a medical empire, contrary to my goals in life. What mattered to me most was a balanced life that complemented my greater goal of helping my fellow man in distress. To conduct a balanced life between these somewhat competitive goals required discipline and vigilance. Medicine is known to be the most jealous of all professions. It leaves little room for other activities.

I moved to Western New York, never doubting I would leave the area once my training was over. Instead, it became my permanent home.

NANCY WITH OUR CHILDREN (1972)

(LEFT TO RIGHT) SCOTT, TRACY, MARK, AND TODD

19. PRACTICE MAKES PERFECT

To establish a private practice of general and vascular surgery in Buffalo was no easy task. Many graduates of University of Buffalo's medical school stayed in the area creating a near saturation of all specialties. In my specialty, legacy played an important role at the teaching hospital, where I planned to practice exclusively. A number of well-educated doctors, (graduates of Harvard, Yale, Mayo Clinic, etc.) dominated the field of general surgery at Buffalo General. Some hailed from established and well-connected local families whose fathers and in some cases their grandfathers, had practiced medicine in Buffalo's tight-knit community.

I knew that Buffalo's medical community was a tough nut to crack. But I also believed any competent, hard-working physician should be able to put up his or her shingle anywhere in this world and make it.

My track record of long years of post-graduate training in the area helped. I was not an unknown entity, and the feedback I received from the medical community encouraged me to stay.

I started my solo practice in close association with a surgeon whose work I respected most. Best known as "Sonny," he had proven himself to be an excellent surgeon with an impeccable reputation in the medical community. His honesty and admirable balance of empathy and clinical detachment had made him something of a legend, and his patients adored him. In certain ways he reminded me of Hemingway. Perhaps it was his interest in hunting, fishing, drinking and his rugged out-doorsy appearance. The only time one found him without a cigar hanging at the corner of his mouth was in the operating room. He even changed the dressing of the patients with his cigar dangling from the corner of his mouth and if occasionally the ashes fell on the dressing of patients, he would remind them that it was sterile, which technically speaking was true.

I used his office to see the few patients I had and covered for him during emergencies or whenever he was away.

He practiced with a group of nine well-established internists in a building with tall pillars on a lovely street with old charming homes just a few blocks away from the hospital. The building was constructed in 1911 as the first medical office building in Buffalo and remains among the historical architectural gems of the city.

The spacious waiting area with the cathedral ceiling and fireplace surrounded by heavy antique dark furniture was reminiscent of a a bishop's waiting room. On both sides of the walk-in fireplace in the waiting room, tall doors led into a long hall with the doctors' offices situated on either side. The offices were quite large, and beside the usual desk and chairs and bookcases, there was a weight scale seen in Norman Rockwell paintings next to an examining table in the corner surrounded by a privacy screen.

Most of the doctors were near retirement age, and a few had inherited their practice from their fathers who had practiced in the same building and had run the medical school before New York State took it over. Though the sons had lost some of the old clout, they still remained powerful in the affairs of Buffalo General.

A colleague, learning I had opened my office at 135 Linwood, told me with a grin, "I hear you have joined the House of Lords."

"Yes" I said. "Although it is more likely the House of Commons now, since I have joined."

Generations of patients had come to the office for medical care. Older folks spoke of the days when they visited their doctors in the same offices as they had as children. One elderly woman described her earlier visit with Dr. G., one of the internists who practiced into his late eighties. After he'd taken her brief history she said, "Dr. G. asked me to get undressed behind the screen to be examined." She did as she was told and put on the gown and was ready to be examined. She waited for a while and then for a while longer. Getting tired of waiting and wondering about the heavy breathing coming from the other side of the screen, she gathered her courage and peeked around the screen to see that the doctor was in a deep sleep behind his desk. "I had no idea what to do," she remembers. "I coughed and sneezed. I fidgeted with the paper on the examination table. Finally, I guess I made enough noise because the doctor snapped awake and finished my examination perfectly and in record time. I guess when you're as good as Dr. G. was, you can do those exams in your sleep!"

Eager to fully engage in my profession after twenty-eight years of study, nothing pleased me more than a telephone call referring a surgical problem. I would welcome such calls whether they came in the day, night, or in the middle of a Buffalo blizzard. Nothing energized me more than being able to pull a patient from the jaws of death or disability. To be able to improve the quality of life in others is a unique thrill.

I jumped out of bed early each day and looked forward to its challenges. Each day brought its unique unpredictable twists and turns. Time floated and passed quickly. When I stepped into the operating room where the patient was covered under the sterile draping, the surgical field became my sole focus, separating it from the face, personality, and emotion of the person. The external world disappeared. My concentration was absolute; my awareness of time and surroundings became foggy and distant. Athletes call it "being in the zone." Some psychologists refer to it as "peak performance." It's a challenging goal to achieve and demands discipline, hard work, and the inner desire to reach it. But that elusive "zone" became my goal and my safe haven every time I stepped into the operating room.

I'd been in solo practice for a few months when another colleague asked me to join him and his group of twenty other doctors considered the avant garde in the medical community, hoping to create a center of excellence akin to the Mayo or Cleveland clinics.

The group shared a building across from the hospital with a nucleus of scientists who would later make a major breakthrough in crystallography and would win a Nobel Prize in chemistry.

In the Buffalo medical community, an invitation to join such an elite group represented the highest degree of professional flattery. When my well-connected colleague, the son of a local surgeon and product of Amherst and Harvard, asked me to join, I did not hesitate and accepted with a handshake. I had worked with him during my training, and I respected him as a surgeon.

The practice of surgery, unlike other specialties, depends heavily on referrals from other physicians. As passionate as I was about being a surgeon, this need to rely on others diminished a degree of the sense of independence I had cultivated over the years. The effort and the maneuvering involved in promoting the self-referral disturbed me the most. In the tight-knit, inbred medical communities where I practiced, one could not survive without steady referrals influenced as they were by ties through schools, clubs, churches, communal activities, and other social connections I'd never had the chance to develop.

As a younger attending surgeon, I dealt with some of the more challenging surgical problems that senior surgeons did not want to tackle. One of my earlier challenges was a morbidly obese woman of over four hundred pounds. She needed two beds in the intensive care unit to accommodate her protruding abdomen. She was admitted to the hospital with much logistic difficulty for an ulcerating strangulated umbilical hernia. (The fatty apron that covers the internal organ was pushing through the markedly dilated umbilicus, and its rubber band effect had cut off its circulation.) Putting her on an improvised operating table, I had to stand on couple of stools in order to deal with her mountainous abdomen.

Every day came with a new, unique challenge.

I operated on many young patients who suffered from the dreaded complications of ulcerative colitis in which the disease could progress rapidly and, without surgery, threatened their lives.

One patient was in her forties. She had three young children and a baby on the way. She had a supportive family, a vibrant personality, and a wonderful love of motherhood. She also had advanced rectal cancer, potentially fatal and in need of urgent care. Her pregnancy could not be terminated, nor could it be allowed to progress because of the rapid growth of the cancer. This was an era when we did not have the anticancer medication or sophisticated delivery of radiation as we do today in order to buy time until a pregnancy comes to term. It came down to a choice: allow the baby to live and the mother to die or terminate the fetal life by putting the mother through a traumatic, risky surgery.

How could I present an option like that to a fellow human being? How could I maintain professional distance in the face of something so immediately personal?

In medical school, I learned about every bone, organ, artery, and vein in the human body down to the last corpuscle. I'd seen death manifested in a thousand ways and witnessed first-hand the strength and weakness and the unimaginable beauty of the human body. But nothing could prepare me to prepare this family for the choice now lying before them.

Although I took great care to keep my professional and personal lives separate, one night over dinner, I asked Nancy for her thoughts. At first she waffled since I seldom discussed such issues with her, and she knew I'd probably already figured things out for myself. But I insisted.

"I have to put her through a very risky operation. She's going to have to lose the baby and live the rest of her life with colostomy. And this is the best case scenario. How can I present this to a young, vivacious mother with such a young family?"

Nancy was quiet for a minute. "You're not just a person," she said at last. "And you're not a god either. You're a gifted surgeon. God gave you that gift to pass along to us. It's your job to help God to help us."

Kathy, a woman with history of a longstanding ulcerative colitis, was another patient I remember well. Kathy was a thirty-year-old emaciated girl almost moribund having been treated for months without response to medical therapy. She had developed acute abdomen caused by perforation of the large bowel.

When I pressed gently on her abdomen, she moaned and opened her eyes. I held her hand and asked her a few questions. Unable to respond, she continued to moan. I spoke with her mother in the hall. I learned that Kathy was a student at U.B. And had been born with deformity of her lower legs.

"Surgery is the only hope of pulling her through," I told the mother. "We could lose her on the table. Chances are that she may have to live with a bag for a while, or possibly for the rest of her life." Kathy's mother's face distorted with pain as she nodded.

I visited Kathy the following day. She was in pain but awake and much improved. Her mother sat by her bed. I pulled a chair up and sat on the other side. I asked her how she felt. "Better," she said.

"I removed your entire large bowel which has been the cause of your problem, but I had to leave you with a bag."

She froze, looking straight at the wall. Her mother held her hand and looked at her with teary eyes, while Kathy stared in silence, tears dripping from the corners of her eyes. I held her hand.

"Remember Kathy, this is temporary, in few months I will put you back together. I promise."

Eventually, Kathy recovered and went back to her classes. She knitted me a white sweater, much too big according to her estimation of my size. I wore it around the house for many years.

While my professional challenges kept me satisfied, my income remained relatively meager. In spite of Nancy's frugality we had to be very careful in spreading our finances with my growing four children.

I had no idea about a patient's financial status or if they had insurance or not. I treated anyone who walked into my office whether he was bank president or a homeless man from an alley. In fact, during my over thirty years of practice, I never learned about the coverage of the different insurance companies and their reimbursements. Nor did I ever use collecting agencies for those who could not or did not pay — except once, very nearly in the case of Mr. D.

Unlike most of my patients who were referred by other physicians, Mr. D. came to see me on his own with an entourage of men and women. He had been seen by other vascular surgeons including Dr. De Bakey's group in Houston for evaluation of an abdominal aortic aneurysm. He was advised to have it removed.

Because of its large size and the danger of its impending rupture, I concurred and asked him why he did not have it done in Texas. He said he wanted his surgery in Buffalo because his people lived here. I subsequently learned he was the king of Gypsies in the region.

Mr. D. was a heavy smoker with severe chronic bronchitis. He had a history of coronary artery disease, which presented a major risk for heart attack. We consulted the cardiac surgeon who concurred that threat of rupture of the aneurysm was greater than the risk of heart attack. And the decision was made to fix his aneurysm first and few weeks later address his heart problem.

The day of the surgery, his clan filled the corridors and the waiting area and roamed around the hospital. Security was beefed up. The surgery went well, and Mr. D. went home after a few days with the usual instructions of dos and don'ts.

I saw him few weeks later for his post-operative check up. He was furious. "Are you sure you have wired me right?" he shrieked.

Stunned and confused, I asked what he meant.

"Every time I have sex," he shouted, "instead of coming out of here," pointing to his genitalia, "I spit it from my mouth."

Choking back a laugh, I explained to him that this was an expected change after this type of surgery caused by a disruption of the plexus of the nerves that regulates ejaculation. I told him that the phlegm and spitting he was referring to was the result of his chronic lung disease due to years of heavy smoking. What I had not anticipated was that a man who had a long fresh incision from stem to stern, would have sex so soon. I had intended to address such expected complications at a later date since we had other life-threatening complications to discuss.

During the course of his care, he wanted me to know that money was not an object and whatever I charged him, he would gladly pay. I assured him that he didn't need to worry; whatever his insurance paid should cover my customary fee. But, when Medicare sent the check for the surgical fee to him to sign and send to us, he kept the check and never paid a dime. I considered consulting a collection agency, but I never got around to it.

Nearly a decade later, my office received a call from Erie County Medical Center informing us that Mr. D. had been admitted there for a bleeding ulcer, and he and the family had requested that I be the one to take care of him.

I read in the evening paper that the county hospital was having a lot of difficulty with Mr. D.'s "clan" who were, as usual, creating all sorts of security problems.

The surgical fees in Western New York were among the lowest in the country, much lower for the same operations not only in comparison with fees in big cities but even with fees in the neighboring towns. Some patients interpreted this as a sign of lesser quality care. Though I had my share of local blue blooded and affluent patients, I rarely heard sentiments such as the one expressed by Mrs. K., an heiress to Kendall Oil.

I knew she was different when they brought her to the hospital. She had her own bed brought in and had the room next door reserved for her secretary. Mrs. K. was in her mid-seventies and wore an opaque lens over one eye as she recovered from recent eye surgery. She was admitted to my service with some degree of urgency for an advanced tumor on her large intestine. Unlike most folks with old money who were unpretentious and unassuming, she was loud and abrasive. During my daily visit in the final days of her stay in the hospital, she was quite upset.

"What is this?" she demanded and waved the bill we had sent her in front of my face. She snapped her finger against the bottom of the bill where the total – a few hundred and some odd dollars – had been printed.

"Why didn't you charge me some round figure?" she hissed. "Something with some zeros at the end! Something in the thousands!"

Apparently inexpensive bills struck Mrs. K. as somehow gauche and plebeian.

Though I shared the unspoken principle of providing quality care with the group and enjoyed the friendship and support of some, I had some of the unhappiest moments of my practicing years while working with the group. I worked hard, covered a lot of emergencies, and took care of some of the most challenging surgical cases. But in the end, I had nothing to show for it. I didn't need a large office and elaborate examining room, since most of my time was spent in the hospital anyway, yet the fixed overhead took sixty percent of my income. I felt boxed in. I was saddled with an expensive, barely utilized office and controlled by a flawed and unchanging referral pattern. And to top it off, without even informing me, the medical group was negotiating with another surgeon whose father was a powerful surgeon with a huge surgical empire to join for political expediency. As one member of the group put it, "It was a marriage made in heaven."

Culturally, the concept of only the squeaky wheel gets the grease was alien to me. I was too proud to talk to others about it. I was critical of my own naiveté for seeing people as I thought they should be, not as they were.

No one in the area had left the group and had survived professionally. Such a move, I'd been assured many times, was the equivalent of professional suicide. Nevertheless, I toyed with the idea of leaving the area and looked at a couple of promising opportunities in California.

"To be rooted," Simon Weil writes, "perhaps, is the most important and the least recognized need of the human soul." It was the recognition of this need, for my family's sake that persuaded me to stay.

I left the Medical Group as I had begun: with a handshake. I was reimbursed for my accounts receivable but nothing toward the building in which I had equal share as a partner.

I moved to the medical tower next to the hospital and shared office space with Dr.B a rheumatologist in a solo practice. In many ways, it felt like a step backward and perhaps professionally and intellectually, it was. Emotionally, however, I'd made a giant leap forward.

Dr. B. was monkishly bald with streaks of white hair on his temples and a pale face with ruddy cheeks. He was gentle, kind, and he genuinely cared for his many arthritic patients. An old-school hands-on physician, he spent a long time with each patient. He helped them get into and out of their shoes, garments, braces, or whatever else they needed help with.

His patients adored him and waited patiently for him in the drably decorated waiting room for their turn, knowing they too would have their share of time with him. Patients baked him bread, cookies, and pies. They knitted him sweaters, night—caps, foot warmers, and anything else through which they could express their gratitude and appreciation. There was no shortage of homemade snacks in the office.

Regardless of the season, Dr. B. was always bundled up in a heavy overcoat and scarf and his woolen Italian racing cap. He left the office well after dark, and before driving his compact old Dodge, he would test the brakes to be sure of their effectiveness and then, with his Italian racing cap on, he proceed to drive ever so slowly and never beyond forty miles per hour even on the highways.

I don't think he ever took vacation or ventured beyond the neighboring states.

He invited Nancy and me to his home one evening to be the guest of one of his loyal patients who had offered to serve a six course dinner for four. We drove to their small, two-story house in Orchard Park and met his wife Jane. He showed me his clarinet.

"Are you playing much," I asked.

He said, "No. I haven't touched it for years."

We sat around a square table in the dining area separated from the living room by an arched connecting wall. The table was set for four. There was a small silver bell in order to call the woman who waited in the kitchen. Dr. B. served us wine in ornate colored glasses. Then he rang the bell, and the women appeared from the kitchen shuffling with arthritic steps and a big smile to serve us a shrimp appetizer. The dinner was delicious, and her efforts warmed the heart.

Shortly after, Sunny, who was contemplating retirement, asked me if I ever considered going back to the Linwood office where I had started with him few years earlier.

After discussing the matter with Nancy, I moved back to 135 Linwood Avenue with my new secretary Nell who had started to work for me initially as a temp.

Not only was I blessed with a devoted and caring wife, I also felt very fortunate to have Nell as my office manager and secretary.

A distinguished white-haired woman, Nell was capable, intelligent, and well-read. She had worked as a secretary for high brass in the army. Nell had come to Buffalo because of her husband's job. Not having any children, totally devoted to each other and their cats, they pursued a stimulating intellectual life. They were avid readers and enjoyed art and classical music. Nell excelled in gardening, and her husband Bruce was a superb cook. Bruce had come from a distinguished family, tracing its lineage back to the Mayflower. His maternal grandfather, Mr. Marcus Baker, a mathematician and cartographer, was among the founding members of *National Geographic Magazine*. During the bicentennial celebration of the magazine, their family was among the guests who were invited by President Reagan to Washington to attend the anniversary ceremony.

Nell managed my office. She took care of all aspects of my practice and gave me a check at the end of the month. By taking over the administrative and business aspect of medicine, which I loathed, she provided me the freedom to focus on patient care.

By leaving the Medical Group, the referral pattern of my practice changed over night. Physicians who had consulted me and referred their own family members to me suddenly stopped their referrals. Though such behavior was understandable in the business and the political world, I found it disillusioning when it concerned people's lives.

My practice began to build up within a short period of time, proving again as I have always believed that when one door closes, two others will open.

20. VISITING REALITY

"The really terrible thing about life is not that
our dreams go unrealized, but that they come true."

— M. Muggeridge

After an exhaustive two-year search, I found a house in East
Aurora that had most of the qualities Nancy wanted. It
drew me intuitively as a familiar place to call home.

Built in 1927 on four and half acres of land, the house was
flooded with light through many French windows and bordered
with blue spruce and white fences. A canopied driveway wound its
way around to the back of the house. In the back, a tennis court sat
in the middle of a grove of poplar trees on one side and evergreens
on the other.

On the other side of the narrow street from the house, low
stone walls surrounded the six hundred acres of a private estate
allowing full view of its rolling hills, charming farmhouses, horses,
and roaming black Angus cattle.

Only half an hour from downtown Buffalo, it was the best of
the city and rural worlds.

The house tugged sharply against that inexplicable spot in me, whispering, "This is the home for us."

Trying hard to temper my excitement about the find after two years of persistent searching, I asked Nancy to come see the house. She did, but did not have much enthusiasm for it. She thought the house was overwhelming. She seemed anxious and uncertain about living in a new house.

Her limited expectations and the tendency to notice and dwell on the negative side of things, a trait I had noticed on number of occasions in past, bothered me.

I was judgmental and saw her as being preoccupied with mundane and trivial problems of daily life, and I grew frustrated with the limitations she set for herself. I felt like a thoroughbred with Nancy pulling too tightly on my reins.

Other times I found myself increasingly reliant on her level-headed stability to keep me from floating off into the atmosphere.

None of this, of course, mitigated my love for her. Throughout our marriage such critical moments have always been overshadowed by the goodness of her heart and by her generous and genuine devotion to me and our family.

I gradually realized and accepted my limited ability to change her views. I began to question some of my own Pollyannaish aspirations. Did I have my feet firmly on the ground? Didn't I need a Sancho Panza to give a balance to my quixotic campaigns? Over the years, I did change, but I have always remembered the saying, "To visit reality is okay, but to live in it is hell."

With Nancy not on board about the new house, I went to a surgical meeting in Minneapolis, still upset. The following day, Nancy called to inform me that she had changed her mind. She would not object if we purchased the house. Delighted and relieved, I closed the deal when I returned.

We moved into our new home in June of 1972 when the old Catalpa tree was one towering expanse of white blossoms. The old tree, with its massive trunk and gnarled branches, stood on a carpet of white fallen flowers, familiarly interwoven into the soft green grass of the early summer. Had I seen such patterns of design and the same color combinations in the Persian carpets back in Tehran?

We have lived in this house for over thirty-five years now. This is the only real home our children have ever known. They were less than four-years-old when we moved in. We have had countless memories in a place that truly conveys the meaning of a home for us. The busy years followed with the routine of daily work and the responsibilities of four children, each with different interests. Scott in tennis, Tracy in tennis, dancing and ice skating. Mark in swimming and rowing, and Todd in mischievous activities at school. Nancy created a warm, comforting environment with exceptional proficiency, and I worked hard to provided all they needed to live a comfortable life with access to a good education. I encouraged our children to grow and excel in what interested them. I did not influence or push them in any direction. When Tracy wanted to go to Nick Bollettieri Tennis Academy, having exhausted the local coaching endeavors, I supported her. And when she felt she wanted to come home after six months, I agreed. I suppose we do project to a certain degree our own life into the lives of our children. Perhaps that is why, on several occasions, I urged them to join the Naval Academy. Mark did apply and was accepted, but he chose not to go. That was one of the only times that I tired hard to get him to change his mind, but he remained steadfast and decided against it.

Throughout the years, many relatives came to see us, and Nancy's gracious hospitality always left them with wonderful memories. On one of the earlier occasion of such a visit, when the kids were small and heard of their arrival, they ran around excitedly squealing, "The Persians are coming! The Persians are coming!"

The accumulating affect of such busy years, which to some degree were repetitious, has left the imprint of some events with the haziness of an old faded picture. But there were others that no matter how often I experienced them, never lost their charm. They have etched my memory forever:

The balmy, blossoming spring days tinged with the fragrance of lilacs.

The hot summer days and the long rallies on the tennis court cheered by the chorus of the cardinals.

The charming color of foliage in autumn, as we walk on a carpet of soft fallen pine needles and gather wild flowers with our children.

Heavy snowfalls that wrap the house like a birdcage and the ice storm that transforms the world into a fantastic crystal ball.

The glowing reflective moments in front of the fireplace, watching the glory of the setting sun over the farm, and Nancy in final preparation for our dinner guests.

Through it all, my outsider view of some aspects of American life remained critical. Among them, the obsessive pursuit of financial security for a safer future at the expense of living in the moment. Working the way so many did, fervently accumulating more and more in pension plans or in bank accounts, hoping to live a good life in the future, did not make sense to me, nor did living the same life over and over again, day after day. There is a Persian saying that "life is not the number of days lived, but the number of days remembered."

A conservative, monotonous approach to life was especially common among my medical colleagues. The majority no longer pursued interests other than medicine. Most no longer played sports, although they certainly talked a good game.

In Buffalo, football plays an important part in people's lives. Monday mornings when I entered the operating room, I could sense from the prevailing mood of the staff if the Buffalo Bills had won or lost.

I attended a Bill's game only once. My oldest son Scott was eight and wanted to see the game. It was one of those bitterly cold winter days Buffalo is known for. We sat on aluminum seats in the outdoor stadium while the snow blew in from every direction. I do not know what the temperature or the wind chill factor was, but it was cold enough that when I tried to stand up, I was stuck to the aluminum bench. I had heard the expression "freezing one's ass" in describing extreme cold, but I didn't know until that day where it came from.

One of the most challenging aspects of my family life has been my relationship with my children. There appeared to be a cultural gap between us, a gap which I felt unable to bridge. While I believe this to be true for every parent, in my case, because of my different cultural upbringing, it may have been exacerbated.

My children thought of me as a serious individual with little sense of humor. They could not envision me as the fun-loving, jovial, and joke-telling young man I had been in the old country. My jokes sounded dull and insipid to them. The deprivation of my childhood perhaps played a role in judging the performance of our children harshly. The hard ship of life that I had experienced, made me over critical of the complacency of the public education. I could not understand their lack of appreciation for the boundless opportunities taken for granted. I could not understand the limitation of goal and unwillingness to take risk, as I witness in public schools, where some of our children attended. Paradoxically the sense of safety provided by life in America also seemed to inspire a sense of complacency. People worked hard, but they rarely ventured beyond their comfort zones.

As part of my upbringing, I expected children to do better in all aspects of their lives than their parents, especially when they had greater access to the tools and means necessary to succeed in whatever field they chose. I thought all I needed to do was set a bar for them and then sit back and watch them excel.

Fortunately, our children have done well, and we are supportive and proud of them. Three of them have been to graduate school, and they have been educated in institutions such as Duke, Amherst, Chicago, Dartmouth, and Missouri School of Journalism. Todd, our youngest, chose a different path from day one and caused me the most grief. Now a salesman, Todd is successful in the competitive business world. He is street-wise, well informed about life, and well-read. Our children share qualities essential as decent, caring, hard-working and independent individuals. And as I have mellowed over the years, I have become less judgmental and critical of myself and of my loved ones. Culturally, the demarcating lines don't seem quite so well-defined anymore.

OUR HOME IN WINTER

(LEFT TO RIGHT) ME, FRIENDS AND NANCY

21. COMMUNITY ROOTS

B uffalo was populated enough to provide big city attractions. At the same time, the city remained small enough to have maintained the sense of cordiality and professional courtesy usually reserved for small town, Middle America.

Through thousands of lives I touched during my three and half decades of surgical practice, my name had gained sufficient recognition to give me the sense of belonging. In name, in family, and in profession, I found myself deeply rooted in the community. I was reasonably satisfied and content professionally by the time the Eighties came around, but I still yearned to grow intellectually.

I spent hours reading and contemplating in the seclusion of my den, a perfect sanctuary for this purpose. Still, finding like-minded individuals or venues for such growth remained a challenge. For me a stimulating dialogue was not only refreshing but essential to a good life. In search for such opportunity, I joined social gatherings where group members received me in their midst. During our dozens of discussions, some members revealed socio-political prejudices occasionally bordering on xenophobia, unaware that I came from the very type of background they were decrying. Most were Buffalo blue bloods, cookie cutter products of the same local prep schools and Ivy League universities.

I joined a waspish club where the upper crust of Buffalo had intermingled for generations and where an Iranian-born vascular surgeon was a bit of an oddity. I remembered well the comment made by one of my medical colleagues a few years earlier: "I am trying to finagle Dr. K. as a new member into S. Club." This colleague in need of "finagling" was a well-established physician like his father, who had practiced in the area for decades, but whose Polish ancestry, in the club members' eyes, set him at disadvantage.

Before formal approval, I was invited to lunch with a group of members in order to get acquainted with each other I suppose, or perhaps for them to measure me as the new candidate. The conversation during the lunch revolved around anecdotes relating to the school days and the jokes of ballroom dancing lessons from Miss So-and-So that everyone around the table beside me seemed to be familiar with.

I remained a member of the club for a few years. I enjoyed the relaxing dinners and luncheons with the free flow of alcohol. Yet, as a venue for intellectual discussion, the experience remained wanting.

My friendship with some faculty at the University of Buffalo, however, provided plenty of opportunity for interesting and informative dialogues. Among the faculty were David Nyberg, a well regarded Ph.D. graduate of Stanford with an interest in philosophy, literature, and education and his wife who, like mine, was also named Nancy. They lived in East Aurora near us, and we shared many dinners and bottles of wine as we engaged in stimulating conversation. David was aloof and introverted, showing little tolerance for intellectual mediocrity. But he was patient with me, and respected my yearning to learn. He helped to fuel my desire to read.

His wife played the role of the friendly private librarian, allowing me access to their large book selections. David and I discussed philosophy and ethics. I ran by him the idea of forming an ethics committee. Always helpful, he supported the concept.

Pablo, another friend, also taught philosophy as a promising junior faculty member at U.B. As a bonus, he turned out to be a formidable opponent on the tennis court as well. Long rallies and engaging dialogue in the serenity of our court were pleasing and memorable moments for both of us. He often referred to such times as among his fondest memories in Buffalo. I too consider them very special.

One weekend during the summer, Pablo brought his sister Veronica and her new boyfriend Kumar to our home. She had come from Mexico where her father served as ambassador from Colombia. Kumar originally came from Kashmir but had been raised and educated in Germany and was now going through his residency in neurosurgery at U.B. After a few games of mixed doubles, we sat down together for dinner. That's when they told Nancy and me about their plans to marry. They had met just recently in a Buffalo laundromat and already had plans to tie the knot in Mexico City. Nancy and I were among a few couples from Buffalo who attended their lovely international wedding, which was held in the Columbian embassy with a Mariachi band and armed soldiers protecting the premises.

Right around this time in Iran, some radical political changes were taking place, changes that would affect my life, directly and indirectly, in many ways.

22. THE VALUE OF A WOMAN'S LIFE

W hen I left the old country in 1960, the United States influence in the region in general and in Iran in particular was gaining significant momentum through its ruling monarch who owed his position to a plot engineered by the CIA and the British intelligence service.

Russian influence within the country was abolished, the communist party was declared illegal, and its scattered remnants were reduced to a barely-functioning underground organization.

With its huge oil and natural gas reserves and over five hundred miles of common border with Russia, Iran became a strategic ally to the West during the Cold War. For the U.S., Iran was a favorite ally and a valued watch dog in the region.

The small groups who were instrumental in both countries for the successful CIA-British intelligence plot continued their cozy relationship by further strengthening the bond between the U.S. and Iran. Richard Helms left the CIA as its director and became the new U.S. ambassador to Iran. Ardeshir Zahedi, the Shah's ex son-in-law whose father played a pivotal role in the plot, became

Iran's ambassador to Washington. His lavish parties, expensive gift-giving in Washington, and romance with Elizabeth Taylor are among some of his legacies.

Iranians witnessed a long period of stability under the Shah. Health care and educational standards in the nation significantly improved. The government built up badly needed infrastructure and introduced a political reform dubbed "the White Revolution." The reforms distributed the land to the farmers, which until then, as in the days of feudalism, was concentrated in the hands of a few wealthy landlords. The illiteracy rate of the country that had been among the highest in the world, dropped significantly. Huge numbers of students studied higher education in the newly founded universities in the country and many others were sent abroad, mostly to the United States or to Europe, to study.

The Shah's appetite for arms and military build up knew no end. This, coupled with the desire of the U.S. to sell the latest technology in exchange for oil, was a political marriage made in heaven. The U.S. showered Iran with the latest and most advanced military equipment and Iran claimed to be among the world's significant military powers.

At the peak of this cozy relationship, over 50,000 Americans representing every conceivable U.S. company swarmed into Iran. For Americans, Iran became a popular place to live. "Many Americans elbowed each other in order to go to Iran," I was told by a high ranking government official in 1974.

During my periodic visits to Iran, I saw many Americans from all walks of life. I ran into Ron Ziegler, Richard Nixon's press secretary, in the Imperial Club where I was having lunch with a classmate. Later, while playing tennis, I heard Spiro Agnew being paged over the intercom.

Huge oil revenues lubricated the rapid transformation of life in Iran. Its traditional life of an agrarian feudalistic society was transformed to an industrial nation practically overnight. Farmers swarmed into big cities seeking new employment opportunities.

Abuse of power and the corruption of the ruling class increased. The gap between the haves and the have-nots widened, further alienating the already-disfranchised. As society began to stir with unrest, the grip of the ruling class tightened, and a full police state under the dreaded SAVAK (the National Intelligence and Security Organization) infiltrated and controlled all aspects of people's life.

Founded by Mossad and the CIA, SAVAK became so proficient that, according to the New York Times, in all intelligence gathering, the CIA adopted a hands-off approach and depended almost entirely on SAVAK.

In spite of a significant revenue increase following the OPEC crisis and due in large part to unprecedented military spending, corruption, and waste, Iran's budget deficit grew exponentially.

In 1971, to celebrate the 2,500th anniversary of the Persian Empire, $50 million was spent for one of the most conspicuous and extravagant parties that the world had ever seen. The celebration, attended by most of the heads of state, took place from October 12-16 in a tent city near Persepolis and served as a showcase for the Shah's modern administration and his social reforms.

Although catering services were provided by Maxim's de Paris and the "Tent City" itself had been designed by a French architectural firm, the French President was among the few major dignitaries who did not attend, saying in an interview that enough of France was represented. And he was right. An army of French waiters and chefs catered the longest and most opulent banquet ever attended in modern history. The highly publicized affair, viewed on televisions around the world, was reminiscent of a poorly choreographed show of lavish superficiality, an embarrassment to many Iranians.

The heavy-handed and oppressive regime of the Shah eventually alienated all strata of society. The nation was ripe for uprising against the seemingly powerful regime, which in reality turned out to be based on a decaying and hollow foundation.

The Iranian crisis, which was badly miscalculated and underestimated by the United States, was a major embarrassment for the U.S. administration since shortly before the regime toppled, President Carter, toasting the Shah in Tehran, declared the country "an island of stability in the region."

The unexpected turn of political events in Iran further strengthened the claims that the intelligence gathering in the U.S. had been corrupted by misinformation from SAVAK.

The Iranian Revolution like other true uprisings such as the French and the Russian Revolutions began at the grass-roots level among the poor and disenfranchised, some with strong religious ties, and quickly swept through the intellectual and middle classes.

Intellectuals, students, and secular groups fell in step behind the better-organized religious groups and envisioned using the religious groups as a bulldozer to get rid of the regime, anticipating a purely secular democratic government. No one expected religious groups to hijack the revolution as they did.

Not wanting to exacerbate an already volatile situation, President Carter at first resisted allowing the Shah entry to the United States. But, pressured by influential circles and by close friends of the Shah, he relented. David Rockefeller and Henry Kissinger, among others, pointed to the Shah's desperate medical condition and his need for treatment as they argued that humanitarian support for an old friend was not only appropriate, but essential. When the Carter administration finally caved in and allowed the Shah to enter the U.S. for treatment of lymphoma, all hell broke loose in Iran. Groups of excited vigilantes at Tehran University, remembering the role American embassy had played in derailing the national movement of 1953, and silently blessed by Imam Khomeini, invaded the American Embassy in Tehran where they took forty-four Americans hostage.

The prolonged period in which both the U.S. and Iran relentlessly manipulated the issue through the media for political gain, was one of the hardest times for me. I cared deeply for both countries, understood the pain and suffering of both, and witnessed how differently each nation interpreted the issues, demonizing each other and chafing their relationship in the process. It was not unlike a child observing his quarreling parents, caring for both, and seeing the right and the wrong in each other's arguments.

My children, who were in their early teens at the time, watched the drama unfold for over a year on an almost daily basis. They seemed confused but asked very few questions. I did not speak about it much either unless asked. How could I explain to them what life was like behind the political scenes? I knew that the truth in time would eventually come out.

I felt deeply saddened by the fate of the Shah. He wanted to do well for the country and indeed accomplished much during his reign. He loved Iran and refused to let his powerful army loose to subjugate the people's uprising. But as absolute power corrupts, he was surrounded by a circle of degenerate, self-serving cronies who isolated and misguided him for their own political purposes.

The Shah, the King of Kings, now a homeless and broken man, returned to Egypt suffering from chronic malignancy of the lymphatic system. His spleen was markedly enlarged creating much pain and discomfort and needed to be removed.

I have not seen his medical records. But I have read the description of his surgery and his post-operative course published by his twin sister Ashraf Pahlavi. And as a surgeon who has done splenectomies (removal of the spleen), it looked to me that he received inadequate care in the hands of some of the best known, but poorly selected surgeons, for his particular condition.

It is quite clear that he suffered from a well-known complication of such operations, namely, "post traumatic pancreatitis." This complication occurs as the result of an injury to the pancreas at the time of surgery. It is also clear that he subsequently developed abscess formation around the pancreas, which was not recognized or addressed in a timely fashion. And when after much delay (due to the bickering between the French and the American doctors supervising his care) the abscess was finally drained, it was too late. Such technical errors, especially the way the complications in this case appear to have been handled, would have been subject to severe scrutiny and criticism in any teaching hospital. The Shah's poor care came down to a simple issue of too many captains.

I am not sure how Dr. Debaky, the primary surgeon, was selected to perform the surgery. He certainly was a world renowned cardiac surgeon who in all likelihood had done this sort of operation fifty years earlier during his surgical training. It doesn't take a great leap of imagination to determine that in the royal court, surface glamour supplants professional substance. Dr. Debaky may not have been the best surgeon for the job, but he had name recognition, which mattered more than hands-on experience.

During the early euphoric post revolutionary days, Iranians brimmed with hope and optimism. Though no one could predict the political future of the nation, a genuine spirit of cooperation and pride prevailed in having achieved the historic regime change.

Most people during the early phase of the revolution assumed that Khomeini, as he had so often declared during the pre-revolutionary period, would leave the center stage and quietly settle in the holy city of Qom without further interference in government matters. But for a nation with the secular majority, Khomeini's lingering presence in governing their lives turned out be a rude awakening.

Changing his tune completely, he imposed rigid Islamic laws as the principal governing forces of the new nation and micromanaged all aspects of people's lives.

In his extensive writings he gave instruction for all aspects of life, from the most mundane daily actions to most complex worldly affairs. He wrote about banking, commerce, taxes, and interest rates. He dictated the scale of monetary compensation for loss of life or limb in both war and peace time. His lopsided principle of jurisprudence showed total disregard for women. For instance, a woman's testimony in the court of law was counted as half the value of a man's in formulating a judicial decision. The testimony of a woman with a doctorate degree was valued as half the testimony of an illiterate man.

I could not believe my ears when my former classmate Hassan, at his home in Switzerland, read to me the following guidelines, which had become the de facto law of the land:

"The monetary value of a right testicle lost in war is equivalent to a woman's life," he read. "In case of loss of the left testicle, the value would be doubled, and shall be the equivalent of two women's lives."

As he read the book written by Khomeini, I could not control my laughter. It sounded so much like a joke to me. As a surgeon, I knew that other than the negligible variation in venous drainage of the two testicles, they were identical, and I wondered how on earth the law favored the left so much!

My laughter over the absurdity of the comical text as it was written in Farsi was soon replaced with sadness in recognition that this was the reality of life in Iran. How, I wondered, could such a regime survive?

Khomeini himself lived an ascetic life in a humble home, but his designated mullahs ruled the nation, heavy handedly restricting personal freedom and imposing a life of alienation for the majority of Iran's secular population.

Most major projects that had begun during the previous regime stopped. The nation's economy deteriorated. The corrupt but powerful governing mullahs abused the system, accumulating huge personal wealth along the way. The disfranchised and marginalized of the old regime were subsidized at the expense of the middle class. The educated, teachers and government workers, were suffered most. The secular corruption of the old regime was now replaced by the new equally corrupt and fanatic mullahs.

In the meantime, the adversarial relationship between the United States and Iran continued. The Islamic government, more concerned about exporting its way of life than about the welfare of the nation, financed and supported the likes of the Hezbollah who were responsible for killing many marines in a bombing of military barracks. The American Navy, for its part, shot down a passenger plane of the Islamic Republic over the Persian Gulf killing all aboard.

Then the United States unleashed Iraq's Saddam Hussein who invaded post-revolutionary Iran on the assumption that the weak central government could be easily toppled. The invasion played right into the regime's hands.

The increasing disillusionment of the Iranian people from the government was overshadowed by a jingoistic defense of the motherland and further strengthened the ruling mullahs.

The Iran-Iraq war continued for eight years. The destruction and loss of life were among the worst in either nation's history.

When the scale tipped in favor of Iran during the war, the U.S. and some European nations, who were supplying Iraq with chemical and biological weapons, began helping Saddam Hussein openly. It was well known by many in the international community that Saddam Hussein was using chemical and biological weapons in this bloody and savage war against the Iranians. But most turned a deaf ear and a blind eye, and no one talked about it.

The war between the oil-rich countries of Iran and Iraq was a bonanza to a number of countries who sold arms to both. No one took great measures to end the war.

The human loss was staggering. Young men and teenagers, equipped only with the plastic key to heaven as promised by the demagoguery of the Iranian religious authority, stood against tanks and walked through minefields. The Islamic regime asked and encouraged families for more children to be sent to the front, and poor religious families obliged.

The media in the U.S. continued to demonize and dehumanize the Iranian people. Naturally, no mention was made of the role the U.S. played in this bitter relationship between the two counties.

The American public knew very little about the behind-the-scenes support of the United States for creating this monster of a leader Saddam Hussein who for decades would be a thorn in the side of the civilized world.

The Islamic regime created a harsh environment for the majority of secular Iranians to live their normal lives. Many escaped to the U.S. and Europe.

I kept wondering how such a regime could survive. In my periodic trips to Iran, I put this question to Iranians from all walks of life. It did not surprise me to hear from so many the depth of their bitter experiences about the strange suffocating life in Iran. I did not have to pry. All I needed to ask was "How is life?" Instantly, the lamentations began about the suffocating life they yearned to change. But when I asked the logical question, "Why don't you change the regime?" They replied, "Look what happened when we tried to change the regime before! What guarantee is there that we are not going to fall from the frying pan into fire again?" Many seemed nostalgic about the "good old" pre-revolutionary days.

My trust in Iranians leaves me with a good feeling that in the end, they will succeed in regaining their freedom. As one of the oldest civilizations, they have proven their ability over 5,000 years to overcome adversity. But, for the new upsurge, they need time in order to recharge their political and social batteries.

The Iranian revolution changed the lives of many among my own family, perhaps none more than my uncle who had considerable power in the previous regime. But the trauma of the political upheaval was minuscule in comparison to the devastating loss of his son.

23. A MURDER IN MINNESOTA

y cousin, Morad, was the oldest of my uncle's three sons. After graduating from high school in Iran, he was sent to Buffalo to study.

Calling from Iran in 1972, my uncle asked me to make arrangements for Morad to attend a college in the United States. My uncle sounded as if all I needed to do was ask the head of the college to arrange for an extra chair in the classroom for Morad to attend. After all this was the way things were done in the old country, a telephone call from his powerful office would be enough to open any door.

Morad arrived a few months later. I took him to Canisius College in Buffalo for his interview since this was his first choice school.

I asked Morad how he had learned about Canisius College.

He said casually, "I sent my driver to the library in Tehran. He came back with all the information I needed."

Morad was a fine young man who was brought up with a silver spoon in his mouth. He was spoiled by a powerful father who adored him. His father Mahmood, my only paternal uncle, was a handsome man with piercing and captivating blue eyes, full of uplifting energy. Thinking about him as I often do, brings back his infectious optimism about life, the love of nature, and his easy laugher that filled his eyes with joyful tears. His spiritual depth attracted many like-minded friends. Mahmood had left Iran as a young man to study in a prestigious French naval academy where he developed the love for mountaineering which he pursued all his life. He was my source of inspiration and the reason for my love of mountains that he introduced me to as a young boy. I think I shared his considerable joie de vivre and the positive attitude in life more than any other in my family.

Morad, after further consideration, finally decided to go to school out West and entered Oregon State University. In his senior summer recess he went to Tehran for a visit and was planning to go to Berkeley for his post-graduate studies. Once back in New York, brimming with enthusiasm and a desire to see America, he bought a van with the intent to drive cross country back to Oregon State University. He never made it. Morad, always willing to lend a hand, picked up two hitchhikers - a man and a woman. With no provocation, they shot and killed Morad, took his van, and left his body by the side of the road.

The police called me from Jackson County, Minnesota to inform me of the tragedy and asked me to come out to identify the body. The murderer was stopped for a traffic violation not far from the scene of the crime. When he presented to police the car registration as its owner and had difficulty pronouncing the name, he confessed to the crime that he had perpetrated along with his pregnant girlfriend.

With the Iranian embassy already notified, the process moved quickly through the state departments, and Morad's body was transferred to Iran shortly after. I received the following letter from the president of Oregon University:

My dear Dr. Sadeghian:

Perhaps you would be interested in knowing that the plaque which was provided by your family has been placed in a prominent location on the Oregon University Campus. We trust it will be an inspiration to all students not only to recognize their obligation to their fellow human beings, but also regrettably as a warning that they should exercise care in how they make this generosity available.

We are, indeed, grateful to you for your intermediate involvement in this process and would hope that you will urge General Sadeghian [Morad's father] to visit the campus of the University at some future time if he is in the United States. A copy of my letter to him is attached for your information.

Very truly yours,
Robert MacVicar, President

Morad's tragic death and the trauma to his parents, especially to my uncle were incalculable. A changed man, my uncle never recovered. He channeled all his energy into the spiritual side of his life. His bend toward Sufism took a new dimension, and he immersed himself in it, finding solace enough to regain his balance and a sense of serenity. But those hearty laughs disappeared, and the vibrant blue of his eyes turned a lifeless gray, never again moist with joyful tears.

During the Islamic Revolution, he was among very few top army officers whose life was spared in spite of his powerful position, but he was kept under house arrest for years. When his health deteriorated to the point of requiring urgent care, he was allowed to go to Paris for treatment for his degenerating eyesight. When I learned he was coming to San Francisco from Paris to visit some of his in-laws, knowing that it could well be the last opportunities for me to see him, I flew out west to visit him. I invited a number of guests for dinner at the top floor of the Fairmont Hotel with its commanding view of the bay, where, in his usual uplifting attitude, my uncle assured me how much he appreciated the view. But, I knew by then that he was nearly blind. Nearly a year passed before

I heard from his second son Farhad that he had been in a Hospice in Paris because of inoperable pancreatic cancer. By now he was in his late eighties and had resigned himself to the fatal outcome of his disease. But he missed Iran terribly and longed to go back. I knew how much he loved the old country. I remembered numerous letters he wrote to me during the early years of my stay in the United States, enticing me by the promising potential he envisioned awaited me in Iran. After further inquiry about the nature of his cancer, I did not think a hospice environment, which is designed for those who have six months or less to live, was an appropriate place for him. His cancer was not biologically that aggressive. I felt he had a good chance of living at least a couple of years in relative comfort. I persuaded his family to transfer him back to Tehran. His return to the land he loved so much helped to improve his health and the quality of his life.

When I visited him in Iran during this period, I saw traces of his jovial self returning. He actively attended regular meetings with his friends. He talked with a chuckle about the symbiotic daily walk with a friend saying, "We walk around the block every day shouting at each other because of his deafness while discussing Erfan." (Efran is the spiritual world of Sufis.) "And I hold on to his arm for guidance because of my blindness."

RETURNING TO IRAN FOR THE FIRST TIME (1967); LEFT TO RIGHT:
MARIAM, HER SON NADER, ME, MOTHER, AND MY DOG PICKY

ME WITH MY UNCLE (1967)

24. THE MEDICAL MICROCOSM

"To know even one life has breathed easier
because you have lived, this is to have succeeded."

– Ralph Waldo Emerson

With my dual responsibilities as the attending surgeon in a teaching hospital and as a member of the clinical faculty of the medical school, we conducted classes for medical students and were responsible for the supervision and training of young surgeons in the residency program.

The dual responsibility of patient care, and training young physicians, created a delicate balance. When questioned by patients who were familiar with the modus operandi of the teaching hospitals, I told them that the residents would be involved in their care, but only under my direct supervision.

Working with a group of younger doctors had benefits beyond intellectual and scientific exchanges. I relied on them to inform me of changes in patient's condition. It was through such feedback that I remained engaged with patients' issues.

I started my practice in general surgery initially, but it gradually changed to mostly vascular surgery.

I met individuals from all walks of life, each with his or her own unique story.

I saw an elegantly dressed seventy-year-old man, an obvious authority figure at some point in his life. He spoke excellent English with a striking German accent. He had poor circulation causing him pain when he walked. It was severe enough to threaten a limb loss. I did a bypass operation for his blocked femoral artery. His condition improved. I learned that he was the commanding general of the famous Peenemunde site in Germany during World War II. And in charge of developing the infamous V-2 rockets, the dreaded secret weapon many speculated would have changed the outcome of the war had it come to fruition earlier, as Hitler had hoped. His name was General Durenberger.

The general was brought to this country with a group of scientists such as Von Braun and others who played a key role in developing the U.S. Space and Aeronautics program. General Durenberger had published a book describing the development of the V-2 missile and the role he had played in the hierarchy of the Nazi regime. In summers he lived in a small secluded Bavarian-like community in the Buffalo suburbs and spent his winters in South America.

One of the more common emergency operations I performed was for ruptured abdominal aortic aneurysm. Since this was a true emergency and time was of the essence, on the way to the hospital, I ignored the ever-present police on Route 400 who always monitored speeders, and pushed my sports car to the limit.

Among such emergencies was a highly respected federal judge with an impeccable reputation. He was in his late seventies, obese and with many risk factors including severe emphysema and bronchitis as well as coronary artery disease. When I introduced myself during a brief conversation in the emergency room, he expressed his concern about the important upcoming trial on which he felt it was essential for him to preside. Frank Cerra, the chief resident in our service at the time, helped me as first assistant. Frank was a gifted surgeon who not only excelled in the scientific aspects of medicine, but also was an astute clinician with a good pair of hands. He later became the dean of the medical school at the University of Minnesota. The judge's surgery went well but unfortunately a few days later and still in the I.C.U., he succumbed to a massive myocardial infarction. I did not know the nature of the trial over which he was to preside, but I read in the paper it had something to do with organized crime. There were rumors the mafia had something to do with the judge's death.

At the time, we could salvage less than fifty percent of such patients. The recovery period for those who pulled through was often prolonged. Survivors frequently did not remember much from those traumatic post-operative days and seldom even remembered who had performed their operation in order to acknowledge their effort or thank them. Though for the surgeon it remained a highly rewarding experience, I must agree with David Hume: Approbation plays an important role in the human psyche.

Another frequent operation I performed involved the removal of the deposit formation in the carotid artery called carotid endarterectmomy.

Such deposits, if unattended, could impair circulation to the brain and lead to stroke. Patients often experience warning signs or transient ischemic attack, which provide a window of opportunity to address the problem before it is too late.

The operation, though not technically challenging, was associated with a rare but devastating complication of stroke either during surgery or during the post-op period. The unpredictable complication occurred in one to two percent of patients, regardless of how well the surgery was performed. This is not to say that a poorly performed operation did not carry a higher rate of stroke.

It did. On the other hand, one could experience a flawless surgical procedure and still develop this dreaded complication, a nightmare for patient and surgeon. It was very difficult to see a patient being admitted to the hospital walking, talking, and functioning normally, and sent home paralyzed or unable to speak. I dreaded the call from residents in regard to a post operative problem when it referred to this surgery. Such problems demanded immediate attention and urgent intervention.

The carotid endarterectomy had gone well. I check the patient in the recovery room before leaving the hospital and everything looks to be in order.

I ask Pat, my nurse, about my afternoon schedule.

She says, "Not bad. Most are post-ops. A few are new patients."

I ask her to put the two o'clock patient in the examining room. I put on my white coat on and enter the room. As I am going through the chart and listening to the patient. Pat knocks and tells me the hospital is on the line. I go to my office and pick up the phone.

"Dr. Sadeghian, this is Tony. Mr. K., the carotid we did this morning, is developing an expanding hematoma."

"Any neurological deficit?" I ask.

"No sir."

"Notify the O.R. I'll be right in."

I tell Pat to cancel my appointments and I leave.

At the hospital, I examine the patient and concur with Tony's assessment. The patient's color isn't good, and I worry about his airway. I tell the patient that he is bleeding and we need to take him back to operating room.

The patient is wheeled to the O.R. Tony, who is the senior resident, and the intern are standing by as the anesthesiologist struggles to intubate. As I am scrubbing, I see that the patient's color is getting duskier. While scrubbing, I open the door with my shoulder and ask the attending anesthesiologist whether he is having difficulty intubating. I know the problem he could be having. The patient is heavy with a short neck and the bleeding to the side of the neck could have pushed the airway to the side making intubation difficult. A few moments pass, and he is still struggling to intubate. I interrupt my scrubbing and ask the nurse for a pair

of gloves and a minor tray (a tray containing just a few essential instruments).
I open the wound. Blood shoots to the left where the residents are standing and
some of it spatters onto Tony's scrubs. I apply pressure to the wound and ask the
anesthesiologist to try to intubate again. He is successful this time, and the patient's
color improves quickly.

I ask Tony to apply pressure, and I go back to scrub. In a much calmer
atmosphere now that the patient's airway is under control, I inspect the site. The
bleeding is caused by a poor clotting mechanism due to patient's underlying blood
disease and possibly aggravated by Heparin, which we routinely give during
surgery to avoid clotting within the artery.

A few years later, I opened my second office in East Aurora
where I lived.

I rented the upper section of an old house that had been converted
into a medical building. A general practitioner occupied the lower
floor. The building was located on the main street and diagonal
from the summer cottage of Millard Fillmore, the thirteenth
president of the United States, who had practiced law in the area.

Many of the folks I saw in my new office came from the nearby
farming communities and found traveling to the city daunting. As
my practice grew in East Aurora, I joined the local hospital where
patients felt more comfortable to go. True, appropriate back up and
around the clock coverage by the residents in the teaching hospitals
was essential for critical surgeries, but for routine operations,
community hospitals were just as good.

Mercy hospital was located at the heart of South Buffalo's Irish
community, where Big Russ, Tim Russert's father lived and where
Tim was raised. The medical staff was close-knit, many were related
by blood, and most lived in the area. The standard of patient care
for less complex medical or surgical problems was excellent, but
beyond the routine, its resources were somewhat limited.

The badly fragmented medical communities in Western New
York created an unhealthy competition between various hospitals.

Many trauma patients were flown by helicopter to this or that community hospital without adequate facilities or expertise to provide optimal care for complex medical problems. This was especially disturbing since the city had built a state-of-the-art trauma center, well-equipped and eager to take care of such patients. There was enough blame to go around. All hospitals were guilty to some extent for such irresponsible behavior.

Despite being a medical insider, I am not sure when I began to look at Buffalo and the Western New York area with the critical view of an outsider. I suppose it may have been present from the beginning, and I had been so involved in attaining goals and overcoming obstacles that I did not have time to notice it.

Puzzling to me was lack of self-esteem and visionary leadership in the community at large. The ruin of the old steel plant, the source of pride and the glory of the region at one time, still occupies a large chunk of premium real state along the shore of the Lake Erie. The area stands today, riddled with dilapidated buildings, next to the grain silos and the elevators quietly lamenting past glory and present neglect.

The self-serving, corrupt politicians reminded me in more critical moments of my old country. In Iran, nothing could be done without greasing the palms of the brazen dictators; here things were done in a more civilized way, through lobbyists and soft money and through back room shenanigans. But even in my moments of darkest reflection, I was well aware of the power of democracy to be able to effect positive change.

Like many young professionals, I had total faith in the traditional teaching of medicine. But over the years, my views changed. I saw how medicine groped in the dark in pursuit of scientific precision. But in spite of encouraging progress in understanding many medical dilemmas, medicine could not claim to be all-knowing. Technological advances were truly stunning, but exclusive reliance on it at the expanse of human input concerned me. We needed technology with a human face.

I began to appreciate the self-healing process that the patient brings to the table. I began to see the practice of medicine as a partnership. Patients heal themselves. Our role as physicians is to help in this process. As much as we like to toot our own horns, most credit really belongs to the patients and to the resiliency of the human mind and body.

The influence of the Cartesian separation of body and mind in medicine did not help the understanding of the healing processes. This dichotomous thinking marginalized the mind and concentrated on the body. And using solely the scientific yard stick, suitable for the body in many respects but often inadequate for the mind, rendered the role that the human mind played in this equation nearly negligible.

As author-philosopher Guy Murchie puts it, "The mind is a universal aspect of life and energy, an aspect with relationship to the body mystically similar to the relationship of wave and the particle."

A positive attitude and even the power of prayer are often unaccounted for in the healing process.

The latest scientific and technological approaches when combined with a sensitivity to a patient's needs, especially the needs for dignity, autonomy, and human contact, are the ideal way to serve each patient.

In my own practice, I noticed the importance of these overlooked variables on a daily basis. I used to perform minor surgeries in the outpatient department run by a practical nurse named Francis who worked in the emergency room when I was a junior resident. She was a black woman with a friendly smile and genuine concern for a patient's comfort and well-being. The rooms were well-lit, the little radio played soft music, and the aroma of freshly brewing coffee made her department a pleasant place to work. I received far more compliments and positive feedback from patients who had their surgery there, not because of the pleasant ambiance, but because Francis never forgot to reach under the sterile drapes and hold their hand during the injection of local anesthetic. She talked with them in her reassuring voice. She occasionally reminded the surgeons of the need for more anesthetic if she felt the patient's discomfort.

I thought we needed more hand-holders like Francis, but the hospital wanted to replace her because she did not have the proper certification. And if it was not because of the pressure from some of us, they would have certainly replaced her with some by-the-book nurse who had a stamp of approval from some bureaucratic technical school.

In the early Eighties, a series of articles appeared in *The New York Times* focusing on some of the thorny ethical issues we struggled with daily in providing patient care. Some of these issues seemed to involve an uphill battle against traditional teachings in medical schools, against the medical industrial complex, or both.

Traditional teaching methods in medical communities, to quote de Touqville, "consistently mistook familiarity with necessity." Consequently, as the sole patients' advocate, well-meaning physicians carried on their traditional role and kept patients alive indefinitely. To some of us, this artificial support seemed to prolong the patient's suffering at a huge cost. It was estimated that the lion's share of medical expenditure in the U.S. was spent on patients who had six months or less to live. At the time, there was little or no input by patients or relatives, no living will, no proxy, and no challenges to the doctor's judgment.

For a democratic society with so much emphasis on individual autonomy, it was hard to understand that when it came to the most precious assets − their lives − so many patients left it to others to decide.

The well intentioned medical community was heavily paternalistic. Physicians felt it was their duty to shield the patients from bad news. To challenge physicians about ethical issues was a highly sensitive subject that raised eyebrows.

I believed strongly that there was a need for a fresh. outsider's look at some of our daily medical dilemmas. By then I had enough seniority and was enough of a gad-fly to convince the administration and my colleagues of the need for an ethics committee.

Not many ethics committees had been formed at that time in the country; the few that had been assembled groped in the dark, exploring uncharted moral waters in search of guidelines.

My trust in idealism and fairness of fellow Americans was further strengthened when I approached individuals for ideas in founding an ethics committee. Every person I tapped, regardless of his or her status in the community, responded with enthusiasm.

To give the committee enough power and weight, I asked movers and shakers on the board of trustees of the hospital to serve. In order to have some guidance, we listened to lawyers, clergy, psychiatrists, philosophers, custodial staff, nurses, physicians, and many others for feedback. Our breakfast meetings started at the surgeon's customary hours of seven in the morning. I was surprised and pleased to see bankers and industrialists and lawyers, people unaccustomed to such uncivilized hours, all attending with a perfect record. We spent a great deal of time settling on the best possible model for our committee. We finally agreed on an "optional-optional model," in which the physicians or a health care provider could (optionally) bring to the committee any ethical dilemma or concern for discussion and recommendation.

The recommendation made by the committee was both optional and non-binding, and the attending physician had final say in choosing or rejecting resolutions.

But since the recommendation of the committee had to be recorded on the patient's chart, the recommendations were invariably followed. Accountability and a paper trail gave the recommendations the teeth they needed.

There was no shortage of candidates willing to serve on the committee. I chaired the committee for few years and maintained my membership until I retired.

At the state level, similar committees began to address some of the same ethical dilemmas. Among these were living wills and power of attorney issues. These were approved by the legislators and became state law.

Ethics courses also became part of the curriculum in our medical school, and with the help of two colleagues, Dr. R. Milch and Dr. Scott Tullman, I conducted classes on ethics for the medical students during their rotation in surgery.

My association with this subject was a source of immense satisfaction and intellectual challenge.

The complex problems posed in our medical microcosm mirrored the problems found within society at large.

Issues brought to the committee varied greatly, but they often as the following case demonstrates, had to do with the tension between autonomy and paternalism.

I was asked to see Mrs. C. who had been admitted to the I.C.U. for advanced breast cancer and a severe lung infection. The I.C.U. staff felt that the severity of her respiratory problem justified intubation and assistance from a respirator. But they could not convince her or her husband, both ordained ministers, to consent. Since I had performed her mastectomy a few years earlier, I was asked to evaluate the situation and speak with her. Going through her chart and discussing the issue with the I.C.U. staff, I felt also that intubation would give her a good chance of recovery. I spoke with her and her husband at length pointing out a real possibility of a normal productive life once over the present crisis. Present during our discussion was one of our surgical residents rotating at the time in the unit. He was an older fellow with a graying beard, an imposing stature, who pursued the same line of reasoning with perseverance and got a consent for intubation. Mrs. C. was placed on a respirator, recovered, and left the hospital.

I asked her a few months later if she could attend our ethics committee and reflect back on her course of treatment at the hospital.

Her testimony was touching and articulate and left a deep impression on all of us. She wrote to me:

Dear Dr. Sadeghian,

Thank you for inviting John and me to the Ethics Committee meeting at the Buffalo General Hospital. I had no idea that my situation was important enough to occupy the entire meeting.

I have always felt that the ethical decisions must be situationally (sic) determined and that there are just too many variables to attempt to formulate blanket rules.

In my case, ethical considerations were made based on many factors, and I appreciate the effort and talent that contributed to the outcome. I also thank you for your kindness to me while I was so sick. As you could see, I feel very well now.

Both John and I enjoyed participating in the meeting, even at 7 AM. The breakfast was lovely and the people delightful. Thank you again.

Sincerely yours,

Pat

Her story demonstrated, for the lack of better term, the importance of the right kind of paternalism. Had we adhered to the strict interpretation of autonomy, without taking into consideration other circumstances that could temporarily distort one's view of the world, the outcome would have been different.

It is with much caution that I use this loaded term of "right kind of paternalism," a term which is inherently biased toward the opinion of the of the decision-maker, and begs the question whose opinion is "the right kind"?

During our weekly morbidity and mortality conferences, a colleague might rally in defense of a poor surgical intervention, arguing that the decision was favored by the patient or by the patient's relatives. I would feel compelled to ask, "How was the choice presented? How was it framed? Presentation by an expert, needless to say, could easily influence the novice. On the other hand, offering a menu of choices in complex issues dealing with life and death and expecting proper judgment by the patient or by relatives is not a realistic expectation either. I think the physician bears the responsibility for effectively communicating his disinterested guidance for the patients to follow. If patients and doctors have a common goal of overcoming a life-threatening crisis, which they do, then pulling toward the same goal should never create disagreement. If disagreement arises, I believe it represents a failure on the part of the doctor to communicate effectively.

The public's high expectations have been a major source of misunderstanding between doctors and patients. The "if we go to the moon why can't we do this or that" attitude consumed much of my time when I practiced. I often had to convince patients they did not need certain surgery or medication, which they saw as an infallible magical cure-all.

The vulnerable public is bombarded by media with false promises of all sorts of medications and cures. The FDA and other governmental agencies are far behind in the meaningful evaluation and monitoring of such claims and products. By the time they begin an investigation, the drug companies have made their profit and have moved on to their next campaign.

Pt. V - Retirement and Reflection

25. HEAL THYSELF

By the late Nineties, the landscape of the health care system in the U.S. had changed dramatically. The new order put less merit in older values and encouraged the cookbook approach set by bean-counters concerned about the bottom line. Nearly impenetrable layers of bureaucracy consumed over twenty-five percent of health care's total cost. Seasoned physicians, acting as an advocate for their patients and seeing beyond the black and white, profit-motivated approach mandated by insurance companies, felt frustrated and unhappy. Many left the profession, and those who didn't, thought about it.

I was especially upset one day when I tried to get permission for an extended hospital stay for a patient insured by an H.M.O. She was nineteen years old, a beautiful young woman, expecting to be married within weeks. She was admitted to my care after experiencing an expanding ulceration of her ankle. She had been diagnosed with rheumatoid arthritis and was being treated effectively with a steroid. But the tiny infected nodule that had started a couple of days earlier was rapidly progressing and going through her system like wildfire. By the time I saw her, the ugly ulcer around her ankle was deep, large, and threatening the health of the entire leg. As preoccupied as I was with sorting out the causes and getting different consultants together and planning proper treatment, I had to call her insurance company first to get permission for her hospital stay. As soon as I got home, I spoke with a woman named Gertrude. I spent a good deal of time explaining to Gertrude the need for hospitalization and my prognostic concern, but I could not convince her to grant an extension.

I put the receiver down, turned to Nancy and said, "I am thinking about quitting medicine."

Nancy, of course, was genuinely surprised. This was the first time she'd heard me speak so negatively. But I was disillusioned. Gertrude had power but was not functioning as the patient's advocate. I'd seen this type of long-distance apathy and ignorance on many occasions. Just a few weeks earlier the same H.M.O., through correspondence by a non-medical bureaucrat (another Gertrude, perhaps) questioned the justification of treating a patient with varicose veins. She didn't even understand the term, referring to it as "a very close vein."

Such repeated incidents of apathy and incompetence, some of which were life threatening and crucial to a patient's well-being, were beginning to weigh heavily on me. I was fine discussing these matters with a person who understood the nuances of medical problems. But to deal with the likes of Gertrude felt like hitting my head against a stone wall.

An uneasy feeling began to erode my enthusiasm for the profession. The pride and joy of daily practice began to lose its luster.

I was approaching sixty-two years old and had been in practice for thirty-six years. I felt strong and at the peak of my surgical career. I had a choice of continuing for another few years in an environment that had been transformed into an unfamiliar landscape, one that was largely controlled by insurance companies who viewed the physician as a technocrat, or to retire with a satisfying career and many good memories. I knew other colleagues like me, guided by a strong sense of personal and professional ethics, who had grown equally frustrated and were ready to throw in the towel.

There were times I had doubts, wondering if I was unduly harsh and critical of the system. But when I heard from the younger surgeons, some of our own residents in fact, who were envious of my retirement and wishing they were in my shoes, I knew it was not my distorted view but a genuine and empirical problem with a faulty health system.

It was obvious to all, the consumers, the providers, and the government who picked up the bill, that the system was broken. I decided to retire from my surgical practice, but since I had been elected president of the medical staff, I still had several administrative responsibilities for another year.

During the last several years of my practice, I was approached on a number of occasions by the nominating committee to throw my hat in as a candidate for election as an officer of the medical staff. The position would lead to my becoming president of a staff of nearly two-thousand physicians. Although this was a highly sought-after position and pursued by the power hungry, I thought I was the least suitable candidate for the slot and refused it. Nancy, devoted as she had been to the institution and working endless hours of volunteering in various capacities for the hospital, insisted and eventually convinced me to go for it.

The two years I served as the medical officer were a crucial time for Buffalo General Hospital and for the entire medical community. This was the time during which many predatory insurance companies targeted financially distressed teaching hospitals for acquisition. Many teaching hospitals, including ours, took drastic measures against the possible takeover by reducing their number of beds and merging with other hospitals in the community to save money. Buffalo General Hospital at this time had an aggressive

CEO who relentlessly pursued this goal. With the help of its board of trustees, he succeeded in merging with three other hospitals, all affiliated with U.B. medical school The cost was enormous. The merged entity, spliced together as it was from different hospital cultures, morphed into a barely recognizable ghost of its vibrant past.

As president of the medical staff and a voting member of the board of trustees, I sat in on all the important committee meetings and observed how this microcosm of the corporate world functioned. I had little if any understanding of the modus operandi of the corporate world and could not have had much impact on corporate issues. I suspected this was true for most physicians serving in such a capacity.

As a person who had difficulty balancing his own check book, I had no idea how they were measuring, overseeing, or evaluating the performance of the CEO when discussion came up in the compensation committee. Had I been a person with adequate knowledge of such issues, it would not have made much difference, since pertinent information was restricted to a select few of the higher-ups. It soon became clear that I served in most committees and meetings for rubber-stamping. The decisions had already been made behind the scenes. I felt like a fool.

I decided to focus on issues I understood and used the power of my office in the area of improving medical care.

There was some concern about the quality of care in cardiac surgery and whispers in the corridors about the higher than average mortality and morbidity rates.

The department was a source of huge revenue for the hospital, and naturally, any investigation could have had major financial repercussions. Nevertheless, I formed an ad-hoc committee and chaired it in order to investigate the issue. Not accustomed to answering to other groups outside their own, the cardiac surgeons and cardiologists were reluctant, and some refused to appear before the committee. My seniority as a surgeon and familiarity with their concerns helped to create a meaningful dialogue and resolution of some of the problems. It helped that I had a reputation for maintaining an above-board agenda.

It was clear that some surgeons were operating on high-risk patients. It took some cajoling to convince a couple of the surgeons that surgery was not a panacea and that it should not be bestowed on every dying patient. The morbidity and mortalities dropped noticeably soon after.

During the years of my practice I noticed a gradual but significant erosion of patient privacy. It was troubling to see how impersonal and robotic patients were treated with no regard for dignity and confidentiality. This new medical microcosm seemed to have forgotten the value of the art of medicine and had marginalized the power of healing within each of us. If the physician's role is to harness this inner resourcefulness to combat disease, then we must pay greater attention to more humane and humanistic approaches in dealing with patients.

Good patient care is an art, emphasizing scientific know-how with a human face. Bill Moyer expressed it well: "In the same way I don't know why the right note from a violin brings tears to my eyes, I don't know why the right word from a doctor can bring hope to my heart. But it does."

No one doubts the giant leaps in medical progress since Voltaire's day, but it is worthwhile to remind ourselves of his assertion that "the physician's role is to entertain patients while they heal themselves."

26. RE-CREATION

I'd been through a lot over the years and had channeled the majority of my psychological and emotional resources into my profession. Now, I wanted a more balanced life. Throughout my practicing years I devoted at least a small part of nearly every day to the study of non-medical subjects that interested me. These were subjects I knew very little about such as western philosophy and literature. I audited classes at U.B. and Canisius College.

Chekhov said that medicine was his wife and literature his mistress. I discovered my literary love late in life. My clumsy flirtation with her began in my late forties when I greedily tried to read as much western literature as I could get my hands on. I even read Marcel Proust's daunting *A la Recherché du Temp Perdu.* (*Remembrance of Things Past.*) It took me almost two years to finish it. Fascinated by his writing, I also had moments of impatience such as the time for example when he devoted page after page to describing the color of a vegetable on the kitchen counter.

In addition to reading, tennis has played an important role in my recreational life. I started playing the game in Tehran when

I was a university student. I played on red clay courts, which today are the site of a mosque, where one can hear the barbed speeches of the leaders of the government as they rail against the west every day on broadcast television.

Through its meditative effect, tennis remained a healthy diversion from my daily preoccupation during the years I practiced. I played with Scott and Tracy frequently, and both became outstanding players during their high school years and dominated in the region. Nancy also played in the women's league.

One year, in the Equitable Insurance Family Tennis Tournament, Scott and Nancy entered as mother and son, and the next year Scott and Tracy as brother and sister, represented the region and played in the finals of the Equitable National Tournament with all the pomp and circumstance of the U.S. Open at the Flushing Meadows. I look at the sport as a wonderful way of getting out into the fresh air to satisfy my daily need for physical exercises, to perspire, and hopefully to exceed my own expectations. I have played in national tournaments in my age group and continue to participate as a ranked member.

One of the most memorable national tournaments was a few years back in Palm Spring where, for the first time, there was a competition in the 90-95 year-old age category. The final was between a ninety-four-year-old and a ninety-two-year-old. They played very well but a referee needed to be brought in when the two players kept losing track of the score.

Along with reading and tennis, I became interested in flying and gliding. I was close to getting my pilot's license. Nancy, who had never stopped me from anything I wanted to do, asked me if I could let it go at least for the time being. She was concerned about the recent number of crashes reported in the paper in the airport where I flew.

I met a researcher at Roswell Park Institute who had been a bush pilot in Africa. Zak was also an avid glider who introduced me to the sport. I loved the bird's eye view and the freedom of the sport, but the weather was a limiting factor. The seduction of gliding continued, and I looked for the opportunity to go up whenever I was out of town for medical meetings.

I was in Palm Spring for a medical meeting, and I called the closest airport to arrange for gliding. As Nancy and I stood waiting for our pilot, we saw this arthritic old man shuffling and limping along toward the building. Nancy jokingly told me "Fero, here comes your pilot." We laughed and watched the man hobble into the building. Moments later he came out extending his hand and introduced himself as John, our pilot! I went up with him and as usual I sat in front and he sat in the seat behind me. The tow-plane released us at the proper altitude, and we started to glide like a bird. Though I loved the silence of the glider at such heights and ordinarily would not want to break the mood, I could not keep my silence out of fear the old man might be dead back there. I had detected in my brief conversation with John that he had a history of cerebro vascular disease and was prone to mini stroke. I thought, *what if he fell on the control stick making it impossible for me to control the glider?* To make sure that he was awake and lucid I kept talking with him and learned that he was in his eighties. He had started gliding at the age of thirteen when he lived in Elmira, NY, (not too far from our home in East Aurora).

I didn't have to worry. John exhibited mastery of his craft by landing the glider ever so softly. His love for life and his passion for gliding demonstrated a young, vibrant heart in spite of his age and past medical history.

After the challenges of the air, I prepared myself to take to the water. I never had much exposure to water sports and was never very good at them. I pretty much bordered on being hydrophobic.

In the mid 1970s, with Nas, Barbara, and another friend Rolf, we covered about three hundred miles of the Colorado River on a raft from Arizona to Lake Mead. The majestic view of the Grand Canyon from below was truly spectacular. I was surprised at the heavy drinking of the crew who started with beer in the morning and got into the hard liquor as the day went on.

The night before we crossed the major rapids, as we sat in our camp within the earshot of deafening tumultuous rush of rapids around the corner, the guides regaled us with stories about boats capsizing and people disappearing into the savage water. Such stories, filled with images of danger and adventure, made the journey all the more compelling and enjoyable.

Years later, my friend Lindsay from Minnesota asked me if I would be interested in participating in their annual canoeing trip in the boundary waters of Minnesota and Canada. I said "Absolutely!"

Canoeing is the love of Lindsay's life. He has been doing it since his early days at Princeton without interruption and intends to cover all the lakes. In the basement of his home, the walls were covered with detailed maps of the region with myriad of lakes. He had carefully recorded the areas he had covered over past four decades.

There were six of us in three canoes. I was the only inexperienced member of the group. We spent five strenuous days in the area portaging and carrying heavy backpacks. I had no idea how to use the oar, but gradually I got the hang of it. We were in the middle of a larger lake on a day with strong winds and unusually choppy water when the middle canoe in front of us capsized. It was quite an ordeal for us to turn around and pull the other canoe to shore. Then there was a severe thunderstorm that hit a nearby tree as we hurried to the shore. The electricity gave me a jolt as my leg touched the metallic rim of the canoe as I tired to get out.

The experience helped me to understand the allure of such breathtaking beauty that had drawn my friend so obsessively. The calling of the loons from one lake to the other as we slept under the brilliant star-studded sky was unforgettable.

With adventures in the air and on the water under my belt, I set out to explore the allure of the open road.

I always dreamed of riding a motorcycle and would have loved to ride one to work. But this would not have sat well with the majority of my conservative colleagues who still associated riding motorcycle with tattoos and membership in a gang. I rode my Honda PC800 touring motorcycle as discreetly as possible, mostly during the weekends and often took the back roads in the farms and hilly country south of our house in East Aurora.

I have had a couple of close calls during the past twenty years of riding. The first one was due to an out-of-control oncoming car. It turns out that the driver was trying to fight off a bee that had flown into his car. The car swerved right at me, and I had to cut fast and wound up crashing on the side of the road.

Another incident, this time as I was nearing Holiday Valley in Ellicottville during a weekend ride, involved a turkey fluttering out onto the road right in front of me. I tried to avoid it, but it was too late. The impact with the bird ripped the side mirror off my bike. The bird then caromed off the side of the motorcycle and cracked against my helmet. I managed to stay on the bike, but I was pretty seriously dazed by the impact and had to pull over to regain my bearings. I managed to get home and, not wanting to worry Nancy, I didn't say anything to her. I asked what was for dinner, (we were almost vegetarian other than occasionally eating chicken).

"Turkey burger!" she said.

Nancy did not participate in my gliding, canoeing, or motorcycling excursions, but she liked traveling in comfort and came along for most of my out-of-town medical meetings. We also traveled to many countries such as Iran, Turkey, Greece, Egypt, Russia, England, Italy, Spain, France, Mexico, and Canada.

After living for a decade in relatively flat cities such as London, Chicago, and Buffalo, mountains began to call to me again. I missed them more than I'd realized. They had been such an integral part of my life that without a return to them, the story of my life would not be complete.

In 1974 I had an opportunity for the first time to go back. The logistical effort to get away from a busy practice of surgery required a delicate balancing act. Not wanting my post-op patients to have their care disrupted, I did not perform any major surgery a week or so before my departure. With each expedition ranging from four to six weeks, money was going to be an issue. Although spending weeks in the mountains took a good bite out of my income, for me, the richness of the experience compensated more than any monetary aspect of it.

Over the years I trekked many mountains including Kilimanjaro and Mt. Everest through both Nepal, and Tibet. I've climbed the Andes, the mountain ranges of Kyrgyzstan and Tajikistan, Mont Blanc in France, Picus Europa in Spain, Nanda Devi in India, Western Ghat also of India, the Canadian Rockies, and the Adirondacks and Rocky mountain ranges in the U.S.

I am often asked what has been the most interesting or exciting among such odysseys. The uniqueness of each region makes it impossible to prefer one over the other. If pressed, however, I would probably choose Everest and Nanda Devi, the former being the highest in the world, and the latter, in my opinion, among the most beautiful.

Pt. VI – View from the Mountain Top

27. EVEREST, NEPAL

I joined a group of physiologists from Harvard to go to the base camp of Everest after attending the 1974 Congress of International Physiologists in New Delhi.

Hotel Oberoi in Delhi was buzzing with American politicians. I recognized Senator Charles Percy of Illinois among them. The Royal Nepalese Airline flew us over a breathtaking view of a fairy-tale land with layers of cultivated terraces sculpted into the rocky side of the hills and where crystal summits poked through the scattered clouds all around us. The sights, sounds, and the scented air of the capital Kathmandu was unforgettable.

The day after our arrival, we drove to the airport to fly to Lukla at 9,000 feet, where we would start our trek. Due to limited seats four of us volunteered to stay behind and catch the next flight. The following day, we flew in a small plane and landed on a strip of rough land as narrow as a bowling alley, with a precipitous drop at the end. There was a shell of an airplane, somebody said it was an old bomber, with broken wings and rusted parts lying in the field. The fuselage sported the logo of the Royal Nepal Airlines on its side.

We met our Sherpas in the "V.I.P. lounge," which consisted of three broken chairs and an open toilet with an unobstructed view of the surrounding mountains. Apparently, a fierce wind had blown away the room's flimsy walls. We were told that we'd be able to connect with our team at Namche Bazar, but only if we covered the two-day walk in one.

We began our walk quickly and continued at a rapid pace, stopping once for a brief lunch break.

In the late afternoon, we reunited with our team in Namche Bazar. One man from the lead group described our reunion: "Suddenly there was a great hullabaloo and a lot of running about in the fog as Fero materialized from the mist at the end of the pasture. Cheers, cries of delight. We applauded, envied, and admired the stamina and speed of the tail group."

The next few days were cold, damp, and foggy with poor visibility. We walked up steep hills marked by prayer flags. The high altitude began to take its toll. By nightfall, the clouds had disappeared and the dark star-filled sky promised our first clear day. In anticipation, we got out of our warm tent very early in the morning only to find massive cloud-covering the sky again obstructing our view.

We continued toward Thyangboche, roughly the same altitude on the other side of the valley. After a deep descent among conifers and rhododendrons and variety of autumnal flora, our winding path ascended up to Thyangboche Monastery. Here, we found ourselves face to face with the great peaks of Everest, Lutse, Nuptse and the most impressive Ama Dablam, refered to by the locals as "Mother's Necklace.".

We set our camp at the foot of the Thyangboche monastery. Mike, one of the younger members who had been having difficulty in the past couple of days, was now clearly suffering from high altitude sickness. David Green announced during breakfast that he had started Mike on antibiotics and that Mike, unfortunately, was not a candidate to continue. David, having reached his own limits, said he would stay with Mike and suggested that the group proceed without them.

Unhappy about leaving two of our group behind, we continued. The abbot of the Thyangboche monastery placed the traditional scarves around our necks. A monk brought out a book, hand printed on long strips of paper pressed between boards, and we examined the drum and the six-foot long horns by the entrance.

As we went higher, the temperature dropped, and the vegetation turned sparse and scrubby.

By the time we reached Phulong, the landscape resembled the moon, cold and barren.

We received the following note from a runner sent by Dave:

"Happy Columbus Day. Mike is better. Temperature 100 degrees orally this morning and a few rales [rattling in the lungs] at the left base posterior. He is quite dizzy, probably from hypovolemia [a decrease in the amount of blood plasma] which we are treating. We are well set up in a little enclosure with a low stone wall right outside the abbot's reception room. We are being well cared for."

Back in our group, we'd reached an altitude of around 15,000 feet. The nights were very cold, and sleeping terribly uncomfortable. I had bizarre dreams, a throbbing headache, and mild nausea, which gradually subsided.

The next day, another runner came to our camp with a second note from Dave:

"I have pressed the panic button on Mike for air evacuation. Further attempts to resolve his pneumonia at this altitude I believe are unnecessarily risky and the chances of his walking out or participating in the congress have now become statistically indistinguishable from zero.

He cannot make the trip unaccompanied and the logical person to go with him appears to be me.....this runner has agreed to go to Periche for 15 R. Lobuje. I have started him with 20 R. in hand."

We heard of three others who were evacuated due to severe altitude sickness. We hoped they could evacuate Mike quickly.

At around 18,000 feet, there were blue green lakes in the crevasses of the Kumbo glacier. Ahead was Tibet. The beautiful cone of Pumori, a mountain sometimes referred to as "Everest's Daughter," hung over us.

Gorekshep, the official base camp of Everest at the foot of the famous ice falls, looked deserted. We had reached our destination.

As we returned to lower altitude, the weather became milder, the sun shone more often, vegetation popped up here and there, and flowering bushes appeared along the edges of a gurgling river. Then there were houses, villages, the laughter of children, and women in colorful flowing gowns working in potato or barley fields as we approached Lukla to take our flight back to Kathmandu.

Lukla was crowded with groups of German, French, Polish, and Japanese climbers, some waiting for days for the flight back to the city.

A plane appeared over the mountins, touched down at the edge of the runway and rolled up the hill through scattering yaks before finally coming to a halt. Everyone rushed toward the plane.

Sitting immediately behind the pilot, I could see how nervous and fidgety he was and how sluggishly the plane gained altitude after dipping first over the edge of the precipice.

He needed to smoke. Turning to me, he asked for a match.

During the three weeks in mountains, I had grown a full white beard. When I arrived in Buffalo, there was thin layer of snow on the ground. Because my plane arrived early, I took my luggage to the side curb in front of the airport and looked around for Nancy who would be picking me up. I was wearing a blue shirt and a vibrant yellow hat I had worn in the mountains. Soon, I saw Nancy with all the kids driving slowly by, looking for me. I picked up my luggage and followed the car expecting it to stop by the curb. But it did not. They kept driving. I started running after the car, shouting and trying to get their attention. They finally stopped and I got in.

Panting, I opened the car door and asked Nancy why she hadn't stopped.

She laughed. "We were all looking for you and when we couldn't find you, I decided to drive around one more time. Then the kids started yelling, 'Mom, Mom, there is this old man running behind the car and yelling!' It just took a minute to realize it was you!"

28. EVEREST, TIBET

In 1988, shortly after China opened Tibet's borders, Mountain Travel, a premier company that organized major expeditions, obtained a permit for a trekking to the base camp of Everest.

Accessible only through Tibet, the east face or Kangshung as the local called it, had not been visited by any foreigner since the Chinese government closed Tibet's borders decades ago.

Bruce Klippinger would lead the expedition, and I was assigned as the team physician.

Reading about the culture, I learned that the origin of the Tibetan people which is inseparable from their religions, was shrouded in myth. Long ago, they believe, Buddha sent his disciple, a holy monkey to be a hermit in the mountain. Meditating in the cave, the monkey heard an ogress crying and took pity on her loneliness (some say she threatened to marry a demon and people the world with their offspring). In any case, the monkey got Buddha's permission to marry the ogress. In due time they had six children who grew up to be human beings with noble traits from their father, such as generosity, bravery and piety, and base one from their mother side, such as greed, envy, and lust. They multiplied and became the Tibetan people.

I read that Tibetans are friendly and cheerful with a serene nature and respect for animals. Their life style is aimed at achieving a harmonious balance between their daily chores and the spiritual forces that they believe to exist around them.

After two domestic flights from Peking, we arrived in Lhasa, the capital of Tibet.

At close to 12000 feet above sea level, Lhasa is one of the highest cities in the world and requires at least a few days for newcomers to acclimatize to its thin air.

In Old Lhasa, we visited Jokhang temple the holiest site in Tibet with its narrow street flanked by stone houses and brightly painted wooden doors where pilgrims inched their way by body length devotional prostration around the temple.

Potala,an impressive building with 1000 rooms, and visible from every direction, was the center of the political and religious power of the Dali Lama. Visiting the inner sanctum of the monasteries was a strange and eerie experience. In the yellow half-light of dozen of strong smelling yak butter lamps, one gazed up at the inhumanly calm and fierce expressions of gods and demons sculpted in huge effigies.

The structure of authority throughout Tibet depended on the presence of reincarnated lamas, monks discovered as small children who were thought to be reincarnation of the previous abbots or lamas and not infrequently found in the families of powerful nobles.

Love and reverence for the Dalai Lama ran supreme and was overtly expressed everywhere we went. His pictures, many of which we carried, put a friendly smile on the weather-beaten faces of all ages and opened many doors.

We were among a select few foreigners to set foot in Tibet after decades of isolation. During our month-long trek, we saw two other groups, one assigned by *National Geographic Magazine* and the

THEY CALL ME FERO   253

other a European expedition that succeeded in putting one man on the summit of Everest

Our group of eight, including my friend Nas, was joined by our Chinese guide Mr. Chin who had been a member of the Chinese expedition to Everest and had lost a couple of fingers and the tip of his nose to frostbite. Another Chinese man named Mr. Jin, was assigned as our interpreter.

We left Lhasa for the Everest region, a three-day trip that covered 600 miles over narrow roads along Tsangpo Valley. We climbed up the passes to 17,000 feet where we arrived at Shigatse, the second largest city in Tibet. Shigatse was the seat of Puncheon Lama and the stronghold of the red hat monks, main rivals of the so-called yellow hat monks of Lhasa. The following day we left for Gyantse, only sixty miles away. That leg of the journey took us all day through narrow high passes. Unlikely as it seems, Gyantse briefly became a household name in England in 1904 when, through a series of rumors, Britain, falsely assuming Russians were given the right to explore for minerals, invaded Tibet.

In Kharta we exchanged our cars for 17 yaks and four yak drivers and gently climbed next to the Arun river along the Kama valley and through passes as high as 18,000 feet. The terrain varied significantly from lush green in lower altitudes dotted with wild roses and tall poinsettia bushes, warm during the day and pleasantly cold at night, to terrains resembling the landscape of the moon. Some valleys were covered with rhododendrons, all white on one side of the valley and all red on the other. Described as one of the most beautiful valleys in the world, Kama Valley is surrounded by giant mountains such as Everest, Lotse, and Makalu among others.

Communication remained a major problem. The mix of English, Chinese, and Tibetan languages proved cumbersome. To communicate with the Tibetan yak drivers, I spoke in English to Mr. Chin who spoke in Chinese to Mr. Jin who spoke Tibetan with the Yak drivers. The end result was a herd of yaks heading consistently in the wrong direction.

On May 19, we reached our destination and set up camp for the night.

The following day Bruce, Nas, and I climbed a 22,000 foot unnamed peak. In this part of the world, any peak below 24,000 feet doesn't even get a name. From the summit, the view of Kangshung was breathtaking. Everest was shrouded in a plume of whirling wind of snow, and ice. Rivers of ice and snow thundered down the mountain into the deep crevasses below.

This was Chomolungma, known to the locals as "the Goddess Mother of Earth."

The rest of the group decided to explore the surroundings of the base camp where they met the American-British expedition. This was the combined expedition that succeeded in getting one man to the summit, truly a historical event.

When I returned to camp and learned about the American-British Expedition and their injuries, I packed our back-packs with a lot of medication and medical equipment and headed for their camp with Nas and Bruce.

By putting one member on the summit of Everest from the dangerous face of the Kangshung without oxygen, they had set a new world record and had done it on the thirty-fifth anniversary of the first climb of Everest by Edmond Hillary. This was a huge victory, and the European media paid a lot of attention to it since the man who reached the top, Stephen Venables, was British. The cost of this success was also high. All members of the team suffered from varying degrees of frostbite and physical and psychological injuries. Our visit, with two doctors on board and plenty of medication on hand, provided a major boost and reassurance, badly needed during months of isolation, and much-appreciated by the members.

Nas and I inspected their frostbite and re-dressed their injuries. Miriam Zieman, a fourth year medical student from Mount Sinai

Medical School and the team's medical advisor, had her hands full and had done a great job caring for her team. Among the four climbers, Ed Webster, a renowned American climber, had the most severe frostbite injuries to his fingers and toes. He physically and mentally had reached the end of his rope. With anxious teary eyes and an emaciated face, he kept looking at his blackened hands and feet as I changed his dressing. I gave him a narcotic to ease the pain and antibiotics to prevent secondary infection. But most importantly, was my realistic assurance of a much less tissue loss as he thought he would have had because of the frost bite. Anderson's injuries were slightly less severe. Stephen's frostbite of his fingers and toes was also less severe, but I worried about his blackened nose. The sense of gloom, thickly palpable in their camp, was much improved after our visit.

I received the following note from Miriam Zieman, delivered by a Tibetan runner to our camp the following day:

May 20, 8 P.M. — Everest base camp

Endless thanks for your support and encouragement today. It was quite an unbelievable vision to see your companions this morning after three months of isolated company, but to find out that two surgeons were on their way down was very reassuring for both the climbers and myself. It was very generous of you to help and advise me. The past few days were exasperating and it was a great relief for me to have you here. Needless to say, the climbers enjoyed your care and expertise and felt better after your consultation.
Sincerely,
Miriam Zieman

Returning from the highlands toward the border of Nepal, we drove through the valleys and narrow gorges where high cliffs enclosed the mighty rushing Sun-Kosi river. Trees grew thicker and denser as we descended. Waterfalls cascaded down the cliffs through the green of ferns and moss. Towering pines trees formed a real forest by the time the roofs of the village of Zhamgmu appeared on the mountain below. Reminiscent of most Alpine villages, Zhangmu was built in the flank of mountain where our papers were inspected by Chinese authorities who eventually allowed us to enter Nepal.

Nepal had changed dramatically, and Katmandu looked sick with its congested and badly polluted streets. Despite the awe-inspiring beauty of the mountains themselves, the city had lost its innocence and the serene charm that I remembered from my first visit fourteen years earlier.

29. NANDA DEVI – BREATHING IN HEAVEN

In June of 1990 I received the following letter from the Mountain Travel company:

We have received a special permission from the Indian Government for two groups to trek the circuit around Nanda Devi this fall. This area of the Garhwal Himalayas has been closed for years, so our trek is necessarily of an exploratory nature. Col. Kumar, who led the first Indian climb of Nanda Devi, is planning and supervising the reconnaissance of this trip. Would you be interested in participating as the physician for this expedition?

Considering it an opportunity of a lifetime to visit this remote region closed to the rest of the world, I readily accepted.

I had read the story of Nanda Devi or "Goddess of Joy," as it is known by the locals, in a book written by John Rosekelley titled *The Tragic Expedition*. According to him, Willie Unsoeld and his wife, on a trek in northern India around 1949, upon seeing the majestic snow-covered Nanda Devi for the first time, promised each other to name their future daughter after it.

Devi, a beautiful, vibrant woman and avid mountaineer, found herself drawn to her namesake. With the help of her father Willie, a well-respected mountaineer himself, she put together a cadre of top climbers from the United States to summit the 25,645 foot mountain. The ill-fated Indo-American Nanda Devi Expedition of 1976, was the last expedition permitted into the area.

The story of her heroic effort in summiting the mountain as told by John Rosekelly, himself a member of the expedition, was truly heart-wrenching. According to him, swelling in her groin caused severe abdominal pain, distention, and persistent vomiting. (The over all picture is classic for bowel obstruction, caused by strangulated inguinal hernia.) In spite of her serious surgical condition, she reached the summit but died shortly after in the arms of her father Willie.

Rosekelly writes:

"They committed her body to the north-east face of the mountain as the burial in the sea. They fell to their knees in the storm and linked hands around Devi's corpse. Willie said the last rites...and we laid her body in its icy tomb to rest at the breast of the bliss-giving Goddess Nanda Devi."

Devi was not the only one to lose her life in this ill-fated expedition: Among thirteen climbers, four others, including Willie, died shortly after.

Since the invasion of China along the northern border of India and the eventual pullback in 1962, the narrow strip of land where the mountain is located had been closed to the rest of the world and claimed by both countries. The sole inhabitants were a special unit of the Indian army called the Indo Tibetan Police who patrolled the region.

I met Col. Kumar in the Hotel Oberoi, the same elegant and charming hotel I had visited sixteen years earlier on the way to Nepal. In his late fifties and in civilian clothes, the colonel carried himself with the authority and command of his military days. The colonel, large and appropriately nicknamed "Bull," reminded us again of the fact that no person had been allowed to enter the region since the last ill-fated expedition two decades ago, and that the exception had been made in our case because of some influential friends in high places in the government.

The group was divided in two; each would start the trek from opposite points. Animals and Sherpas would be provided from the villages along the way to help carry gear and supplies over passes averaging 19,000-feet high. The two groups would meet at a designated plateau on the other side of their respective passes where they would exchange animals and Sherpas. They would then continue the circuit to the end. This would allow the Sherpas and the animals to return back to their own villages. I was assigned to group A; a younger orthopedic surgeon from San Francisco was the physician for group B.

Leaving at five in the morning, our bus crawled through the crowded streets of New Delhi. Many who had slept on the narrow benches in the streets remained curled up and immobile. Others woke up standing and yawning. Some squatted in front of a small wood fire and prepared for breakfast. By the time the purple-pink of the cloudless sky had changed to orange-red, our bus was well into the countryside crawling slowly toward the lower hills of the Himalayas and a village called Rishikesh where we would be staying over night.

We drove along the banks of Ganges River, an integral part of Hindu life. The river's edge was crowded with people, all totally absorbed in their rituals, pouring water on their heads with cupped hands and whispering prayers. Pilgrims in vibrant colors of white, saffron, yellow, and red filled the sacred temples along the banks of the river. The ornamented saris of the women and the equally colorful turbans of the men, created a rainbow of humanity through which, sacred cows, monkeys, cats, and dogs freely moved. Dark shops were flanked by flowering bushes and trees full of exotic, chirping birds. In the street, the vendors, snake charmers, and men with long beards and painted faces squatted on the curbs. Unable to find my hat and needing a head cover against the blazing sun, I knotted the four corners of my bandanna and placed it on my head. With my dark skin and my growing beard, I blended right in.

The unceasing pageantry of the transparent life in India has never lost its charm for me. I was mesmerized.

We reached Rishikesh and camped on a hill-top at dusk. The small shops were lighted by candles, oil or hurricane lamps, and a few by dim electric bulbs. The Ganges flowed calmly under the soft blue sky of the setting sun. The rattle and chatter of daily life fell silent, the river's whispering current reaffirming the harmonious flow of life.

Journal Entry — Oct. 6, 1990

I stayed in camp most of the day waiting for permits and other bureaucratic hoops required by the Indian government. There are apparently many big cats roaming the area which explained the reason for the metallic collars with sharp spikes around the necks of the dogs in the nearby village. I ran into a pack of monkeys early in the morning alone as I went down to the river to wash. The females carried their young on their backs, and the males looked at me suspiciously.

Later while washing my hair by a small waterfall, a young family came and stood by, watching me. The mother, herself a child, perhaps 15 or 16, quite attractive with beautiful eyes and soft smooth skin, held the hand of her young son and daughter. The father stayed back. He did not speak. The mother asked if I wanted to take her son. I asked jokingly, "What about your girl? She said quickly, "Okay. Take them both."

Hardish, our designated Indian leader, and a liaison army officer joined us. Hardish was born in the region but had left his village after the Chinese invasion. He was well credentialed, having many climbs with Indian expeditions under his belt including the Everest expedition of 1965.

Our trek would begin in Liam, an army post at 11,000 feet, where a small number of (ITBP) Indo-Tibetan Border Police were stationed. The last eight kilometers to Liam was a narrow road carved against the mountain. Leaving our bus, four of us crammed into the front seat of an Indian army mini-truck, with the rest seated in the back on the two benches. The truck crawled the steep switchbacks and after a sudden noisy shift of the gears, the driver announced we had no clutch. Reejo, one of our guides, tried to engage the truck into low gear while three of us, including the driver, stood and watched. By some miracle, the gear engaged, and the truck started moving. Running and scrambling, we all managed to get in the front seat where Reejo was now in control of the steering wheel with the military driver controlling the gas pedal and brakes. The truck reached the end of the road, and, moaning loudly, heaved to a stop.

Narrow paths traversed the high rocky gorges where the army had placed fixed ropes in some of the more exposed areas known for fierce winds. We spent the night in Liam, an Indian army barracks.

Ready to begin our trek, we were joined the following day by a group of Sherpas and over thirty horses.

It soon became very clear that no one, including our leader, who came from the other side of the pass, had any knowledge about this region. There were no reliable maps, and those provided by the Indians were hopelessly inadequate. The only realistic source of accurate information came from the ITBP, which guarded the area sporadically and considered us suspiciously in spite of all the assurances given us by several high-ranking army officers in New Delhi. We could not take any photos, and our cameras were confiscated. Hardish, along with two other locals, went ahead for reconnaissance of the terrain ahead.

The night before going over the pass, Janine, a Marathon runner in her thirties from California had difficulty coping with the altitude. Her resting pulse rate of 100 and her foggy mental status worried me. I sent her down to the lower level with a few Sherpas to connect with Group B and return to New Delhi.

Others in the group were also affected. As the de facto leader of the group since Hardish had gone ahead for reconnaissance, I advised the group to stay another night before going over the pass.

Journal Entry

As I am writing this, my tent mate is discussing in detail how people have been missing or not aiming properly at the hole we dug as our toilet and how a glob is stuck to his boots. Everyone seems to be experiencing gastroenteritis, and the mood is decidedly somber. The only cheerful person in camp is our Nepalese assistant who sings greetings to everyone. He speaks to me often using the only English word he knows: "Okay!" Every time he sees me, he engages me in an animated round of dialogue, something along the lines of, "Okay! Okay! Okay! Okay!" This pleases him immensely, and he beams his toothy smile at the rest of the porters, proudly showing off his conversational skills.

Most members of the group were experienced, high-altitude trekkers, but a few, and one couple in particular, had a tough time going over the pass. They were physically and psychologically drained and needed a lot of help throughout. I had my hands full. At one point I had to carry the woman for a while on my back. To help them, I stayed at the end of the trail to be sure they were all right.

We met Group B as planned on a flat plateau after descending from our respective high passes. They'd had their share of problems, too. In addition to some with acute mountain sickness, one woman had suffered a stroke. She had been carried out on a horse but had subsequently fallen and suffered multiple bruises and fractured ribs. I found her lethargic in her tent with some neurological deficit in the form of facial paralysis. I started her on intravenous fluids and aspirin and called for immediate evacuation. She was evacuated by helicopter to New Delhi shortly after.

Stroke and swelling of the brain are not uncommon at high altitude. Also common is the leakage of fluid in the lungs and a whole host of other problem caused by dehydration.

Unlike the arid side of the pass that we had covered, this side of the pass was lush and green. Magnificent valleys and deep gorges cradled torrential rivers with an array of flowering bushes and trees from the familiar to the exotic. There were many waterfalls cascading through high vertical cliffs and immense lush hills forming the tributaries of the Ganges. With such an abundance of exotic flora and fauna, untouched by human hands, it looked for all the world like heaven on earth.

Taking advantage of the slow pace of the couple who continued to have difficulty keeping up with the rest of the group, I walked behind them, intoxicated by the beauty of nature, my eyes moist with tears of joy, grateful for the chance to experience this paradise, when I heard Larry ask, "How much further?"

"Not much more," I said. "We're almost there."

"This is like a death march."

I didn't respond, but it occurred to me how far apart my world was from his. At the exact moment I was breathing in Heaven, another man just a few feet away was choking in Hell.

We reached the uninhabited village of Milam where our guide Harish was born and where his family subsequently fled after the Chinese invasion. We took a tour of the empty but charming village with its stone houses. Harish showed us the homes of his father who was village chief and of his wife before they were married. We saw a courtyard with a tree in the middle, a kind of gathering place, a court house, he said where village elders used to settle disputes.

Before our arrival it had begun to snow, and the entire village was now covered with thin layer of snow punctuated incongruously by a perfusion of wild flowers lifting their colorful heads up above the flakes.

Harish told me about a rare, special herb that grew in and around his village. Soon he found a bunch. It looked and tasted like a common chive to me, but I didn't have the heart to tell him we had the same thing in plentiful supply back in the States.

As we descended, hamlets began to appear. Children with happy, curious faces ran and giggled along the track holding the palm of their hand up saying the traditional greeting of "Namaste," and scuttled off amid a flurry of giggles.

After checking our belongings with the military at Bugdiar, we proceeded on to Munsyarie. I saw a very old man struggling along the steep path with his equally old, badly-emaciated, blind, and arthritic donkey. The donkey carried a light bundle and had to rest every few steps along with his old master. I wondered how long this partnership had existed, and how much longer it would last.

The group cheered loudly at the sight of our army truck waiting in the distance to take us to Munsiyari.

Here I visited the medical clinic. Once the village learned there was a doctor on hand, my impromptu mountain medical practice grew rapidly. I saw the wife of the mayor in a well-to-do house. She suffered from chronic peptic ulcer. In another home, I saw a severely burned young man with scarring of his lips and face and in bad need of a re-constructive surgery. I was asked to write a letter and certify the need for such surgery. I wrote the letter, although I had no idea to whom my recommendation would be given or if it would even be understood or followed. In another home, I saw a young girl with enlarged lymph nodes caused by tuberculosis. A young member of the Indian army seeking medical advice was brought into my tent with acute mountain sickness.

Leaving the village by bus, we drove on the winding roads for two long days that coincided with Diwali, a special Hindu celebration during which people decorate and illuminate their homes, shoot off fire crackers, eat sweets, and stay up late at night.

30. RETIREMENT – THE NEW BEGINNING

"When the world has the way, running horses retire to till the field."

— Tao

Nancy was reluctant to support my idea to retire. We had heard plenty of stories from the wives of retired colleagues about the extra friction retirement created in their married lives.

Nancy was also concerned about how I would cope with life as an Ordinary Joe.

She said, "You won't be a working doctor anymore. How will you handle not being up on that pedestal?"

It was a good question.

I was certain boredom would not be a problem. The decision to leave medicine was difficult. After a lot of soul searching I thought it was an appropriate decision at this juncture of my life. And once I'd made my decision, I looked forward to retirement with eagerness and with the same anticipation I had felt after graduation from high school, wondering what lay around the corner in this new phase of my life.

Though my introspective bent stressed the importance of living in the moment, the demands of professional life during my busy practice always got in the way. Every daily task took a back seat to my professional activities. I listened to the news superficially and participated in social activities halfheartedly. I finished meals in a rush, always eager to get back to work. Even on the tennis court, my mind could not be totally focused on the game. I slept with one eye open, ready to spring into action if needed. I had forgotten all about a peaceful uninterrupted sleep and my dreams were a jumble of daily professional activities.

Since retirement, the vibrant dreams of my younger years have began to trickle back. I enjoy doing simple tasks. I laugh a great deal at myself and at the silly mistakes I make. I am not as self-critical or judgmental about others. I sing melodies of the old days, wondering where the songs are coming from. I am not as tense on the tennis court. My game has even improved. I enjoy the freedom of anonymity, of being called by my first name. I don't use my title anymore.

When colleagues who are approaching retirement age ask how I am coping with the retirement and wondering if they should consider it, I tell them that retirement is not for everyone. Each person needs to evaluate his or her own unique situation. I have seen some very unhappy doctors who do not know what to do with themselves when they retire. Such individuals are so absorbed in medicine that once that is taken away from them, they feel lost and wither away from boredom. I also know many octogenarians, who in recognition of this fact, continue in their medical practices relatively happy.

Retirement needs preparation. The prevalent assumption of working hard, stopping completely one day, and picking up the golf clubs the next and traveling happily ever after is a common mistake that has disillusioned many.

Since my retirement, I have been spending more than six months on Amelia Island just off the northeastern coast of Florida. I could not be happy trapped in yet another Buffalo's long winters. It didn't matter when I worked. In the operating room, I wasn't aware of the weather or the time of the day. But in my retirement, I need the sunlight.

The Island is one of the southern chain of barrier islands that stretches along the east coast of the United States from South Carolina to Florida. It is twelve miles long and four miles wide with a colorful political history of being ruled under eight different flags. The sleepy, almost unknown Island was gem of a natural beauty with miles of wide sandy undeveloped beaches when I bought my Pied a Terre in 1982. Half a mile south of us was the historical site of the American Beach, founded in 1935 exclusively for black Americans by a black millionaire Mr. Lewis. The slow pace of the island has an unmistakable calming effect on me. I am drawn by its relaxing southern charm, by its canopied streets adorned with Spanish moss, where, the traffic signs warn you to beware of the passing peacocks.

It is on the balcony of my bed room where I wait every day to greet the rising sun from the middle of Atlantic. In such moments, I am not alone, the birds have been singing in anticipation of it for a while.

The fact that I have been coming to the island for nearly thirty years, makes me one of the old-timers. I have met many new friends and acquaintances and seem to be developing roots here. I have continued to study French here, a new language which I started after retirement eight years ago. The class is conducted by a dynamic retired French teacher who originally is a New Yorker but now lives on the plantation. There are seven of us in the class, all women, beside me and Buster, the teacher's white poodle. The class is humming along. We have started reading literary authors, among them many of Maupassant's short stories.

Amelia didn't stay the same too long, ten years ago, the Ritz Carlton built one of its flagships next door and since then, the island has been put on the map with a lot of new construction.

Golf and tennis are big in the island, providing opportunity to keep my skills up. I play at the Ritz, Surf and Racquet Club or Plantation locally and have continued to play in the national tournaments in my age group.

My retirement from the busy medical profession has provided me with frequent opportunities to ride my motorcycle.

I arranged through a local company in Auckland to take a tour of New Zealand covering both islands. The tour company provided the motorcycle, proposed my itinerary, and made arrangements for bed and breakfast during my stay in different locations. The first three days, I joined a group of Germans for the tour of the north island. The Germans were avid bikers. They came with leather racing gear and curvy women. They also loved the curves of the roads.

Between severe jet lag, a new motorcycle, getting used to driving on the wrong side of the roads, and trying to keep up with speed crazy Germans, the first few days were, to say the least, challenging. On more than one occasion I found myself facing an oncoming car. I seriously questioned my judgment. I thought I had made a bad decision, and I came close to giving it up altogether. But, once the solo part of my tour began, things improved. The following two weeks, I toured the shores and the mountainous region of north and south islands alone, and on my own pace. The experience was pure pleasure. Other than a powerful storm on the day of traversing the Cook straight the weather cooperated, and the sun shone most of the time. Staying in bed and breakfast lodging provided an excellent chance to get to know the culture more intimately. New Zealand reminded me in many ways of old England, although it surpasses England by far in terms of pure, natural beauty.

It was shortly after my retirement that I began to write this memoir. I had never written before. The only time I came close was when I falsely claimed to be a professional writer a few years back in Tajikistan:

We had gone to Russia shortly after the fall of communism to trek in the mountains of Tajikistan. This was during the time that Russia was fighting in Afghanistan, just on the other side of the mountains.

Returning from the mountains, we stayed in the only hotel in Dushanbe (capital of Tajikestan) rumored to be full of CIA, KGB, and Iranian revolutionary agents. It was reminiscent of the movie Casablanca, full of intrigue and uncertainty. As I was coming out of the elevator I met this chap in a safari uniform. He looked like he'd just come from hunting elephants in the Serengeti. I suppose I looked just as odd to him with my grisly beard and unwashed weeks of mountain clothing and my confusing accent. He asked me in his clumsily exaggerated British accent, good day sir, what are you doing here? I said you first sir, what about you? He said he was there to support the fighters in Afghanistan. I said I was a writer. I did not tell him that I wrote prescription and left it with that.

Writing of this memoir has taken a good bit of my time. As challenging as I have found writing this memoir, it has also given me the tremendous pleasure of reliving the moments of past.

Kanchanjunga was my last major expedition, the year was 2000, and I had just turned sixty-five.

WITH OUR CHILDREN ON AMELIA ISLAND (LEFT TO RIGHT: TRACY, TODD, ME, MARK, AND SCOTT)

ME WITH MY LOYAL PC800

31. THE FIVE TREASURES

In the fall, I joined a small group to trek into Kanchenjunga region. Ibex Expedition, owned and operated by Bruce Klippinger was in charge of the logistics.

Entering Hotel Malla's lobby in Kathmandu, I saw Bruce coming toward me with the same smile, not changed much, perhaps his hair a little whiter since our last mountaineering of the northeast face of Everest in 1988. We hugged, genuinely pleased to see each other

Our itinerary called for spending a month in the area. The massive mountain range has five separate peaks hence its name "Kanchenjunga," meaning "the Five Treasures of snow." The region forms the eastern border of Nepal where the mountains separate Nepal from Tibet in the north and Sikkim in the east. During the four-week expedition, we would be covering about 250 miles of rugged territory with many ascents and descents and some passes as high as 19,000 feet.

I met the rest of the group: Bob and Laurie from New Jersey; Bruce, Charlene, and Kelly from Boulder, Colorado; David and Barbara from New York City, and Tom from California.

We boarded an ancient World War II plane with a newly-painted knife on its tail, an emblem of Gurka Airline. The low-ceilinged plane had the capacity for 18 and came with a stewardess who had to bend in half at the waist to serve us frequent candies. In Bratnigar, we met Norbu our "sirdar" who would be in charge of the camp logistics. Norbu placed the customary white scarf around our necks, a Buddhist talisman to protect us from accidents.

Norbu was about forty-five, with a toothy pleasant smile which quickly disappeared when he got down to the business of instructing the crew. He spoke English reasonably well and was curious about the customs and the way of life in the West. He carried a small pad of paper with him and jotted down English words from time to time. Norbu had originally come from Tibet as a porter and had worked his way up to this highly sought after position as a sirdar.

Because the paths of our trek were narrowly carved into the side of the mountains, using pack animals was out of question. Instead we had a crew of sixty Sherpas, each with a specific job. The stove man got up at 5 A.M. to boil enough water for the camp. At 6 A.M. members of the kitchen crew went from tent to tent offering coffee or tea. The lowest on the crew's totem pole were barefoot teenagers who carried some of the more heavy loads. A demanding hazardous job with possibilities of serious injuries and even death.

In the afternoon, our Tata, a ubiquitous Indian-made bus arrived. The driver was a wild-eyed native man, decked out in blue jeans, earrings, and garishly cheap shades. He drove us recklessly through the city with his bus horn blaring from start to finish. As in India, horns aren't just a signal to cows, goats, and buffalo to get out of the way: They are a means of communicating with other drivers and pedestrians. A screeching horn blare might mean anything from "Hello" to "I'm merging now" to "Move your butt!"

I was relieved when we reached a dirt road and our driver was forced to slow down and give his horn a rest. The cost for our relief though was no bargain. Soon the boxy Tata with its huge wheels and high center of gravity started pitching from on big pothole to the other. Monsoons in Nepal raise havoc with dirt roads and repair efforts are few and far between. For the entire ride, we rolled violently from side to side and jerked in every direction. Dirt kicked in through the Tata's broken windows, and a film of dust formed on my sunglasses. All the while, the road steepened, and the Tata struggled up.

At around 8 P.M., we finally stopped and walked with the aid of a flashlight to our campsite.

I woke up in the middle of the night to the barking of dogs. The roosters crowed soon after.

In the morning, the saga of our rolling Tata continued. The weather remained hot and the dust thick. The constant babbling of the crew in the back of the bus in mixed languages of Nepalese, Tibetan, Chinese, and Indian mingled with the loud Indian music from our driver's single cassette tape. Not to be outdone, Tata added her metallic grinding song from the rough and rocky road.

We reached the campsite after another nine hours of driving and caught our first glimpse of the Kanchenjunga. The white massive peak stood alone, far away in the horizon and beyond numerous green hills in the foreground.

I woke up at 4:30 A.M. to the crowing of roosters from the nearby village. Shortly after, a group of children came and started singing. I got out of my tent. It was still dark and I could not see the children well, only heard them running from one bush to another. The children's songs were lyrical, and their voices clear and beautiful. I kept shining my flashlight in their hiding area in sort of a hide and seek game as they led me by song from one of their hiding places to the next. As, morning arrived, the group, a mix of boys and girls all around the age of ten or eleven, became visible. They darted around playfully in their school uniforms, still singing, until they faded along with their voices in the distance.

As we started our trek, Bruce D., struggled to put on his back pack. Finally set, he took a few wobbly steps and slipped face-first into a clump of steaming cow dung. Unfazed, he stood, wiped himself off, and said to his wife, "Hardly an auspicious start. I hope it's not a sign."

The path swerved and undulated among low hills, among tea plantations, and along the many terraced hills and cultivated rice paddies. The trail climbed over ridges and plunged down to a valley and a roaring river.

Along the way, various small villages appeared. As I climbed the narrow path, the roaring river formed a long, silky blue ribbon meandering among the green valleys.

Walking alone, as I try habitually do in mountains, I passed a small yard that was crowded by three generations of the same family working around a heap of harvested rice, a delightful scene for a painter or a photographer, and, not being either, I stopped to absorb as much of it by visual memory as I could.

One of the boys, probably in his late teens, walked up to me and asked, "Do you want me to show you a trick?"

I said, "Sure."

He bent over, kicked his legs into the air, and proceeded to walk around on his hands.

I applauded, and others in the yard followed suit, saying "Namaste!" and congratulating the young man on his gymnastic prowess, I hurried to catch up with the rest of the group.

To appreciate the mountains I needed to be alone. I've always needed that solitude to better hear, see, and memorize the moments. I suppose it goes back to my younger days of spending time alone in the Alborz range. Such moments facilitate access to my intuitive feelings and help me to understand who I am. I can't seem to gain that same degree of internal spiritual access while in the company of others. In my diary I wrote:

"Demanding walk in a beautiful countryside. To describe the beauty of this terrain, no matter how skillful a writer, cannot do justice to the experience itself. An attempt by a novice is shockingly inadequate."

The weather remained warm and sunny as we climbed massive hills and down to the roaring valleys. The food was superb, the best I have had in any expedition, thanks to our cook who had been a chef in a reputable hotel in Kathmandu.

In another entry in my diary:

"I wish I had recorded my wonderful dreams. Another strenuous day of hiking, to sleep in fresh crisp cold surroundings of higher elevation in the warmth of my sleeping bag is a perfect recipe for good dreams."

A few days later, after dinner we sat in front of our tents with dozens of villagers gathered around us. The village women put flowers around our necks. A local drink called *rakshi* flowed freely among the crew. The circle of the villagers grew. A big official came, sat on a chair next to us, and was offered *rakshi* and flowers. Soon, singing started, and young girls began to dance. Older women joined them and then men joined in from our crew of Sherpas. Then they asked us to participate, and the villagers laughed and cheered us on. The ringleader of the local group played a harpsichord-like instrument and spoke and sang in garbled English. Norbu demonstrated his mastery in dancing. It did not surprise me. I thought he belonged to that subgroup of our species blessed with so much enthusiasm and zest for life, that his performance, no matter what he did, easily surpassed all others.

We approached the south base camp at an altitude of 15,000 feet and the scarcity of oxygen began to affect us.

Bob had difficulty breathing, and I worried about his slow irregular heart beat. Tom, (an intensive-care physician) and I agreed that it was too risky for Bob to continue and sent him down with group of Sherpas to be evacuated.

The following day Bruce K, Barbara, Tom and I left for a four-hour walk above the base camp when to my surprise, breathing very hard pushing herself to the limit, Kelly came along with the help of two Sherpas. I admired her determination but felt her judgment was inappropriate and she could regret it later.

She panted, "I paid a lot of money to see this, and I'm going to see it."

Next day we started on unmarked piles of boulders traversing the rocky mountain to the left leading up to the pass. Exposed areas with an unstable footing made our progress difficult. I reached the ridge around noon, finding Tom and Barbara already there. All of us felt the scarcity of oxygen. It was an exhausting climb. Tom pulled out an oxymeter from his bag. After attaching it in turn to each of our forefingers, he reported that we all had a low enough oxygen saturation to be candidates for admission to the I.C.U for intubations and use of a respirator.

It was comforting to see the clear and cloudless sky for the day of our climb over the pass; any precipitation could have created a major deterrence to our progress. Ascent of the treacherous path and the long precipitous descent under icy and snowy conditions would have been sure ingredients for disaster. Around November and in these high altitudes, the weather could turn rapidly, and accumulation of considerable snow in a short time was not unusual. We risked being stranded by the weather at any time.

Kelly, drained and exhausted, was carried up the ridge by two porters.

Descending from the pass was tough; the terrain varied and remained unstable. David started having trouble with his knees and was assisted by Norbu and other Sherpas all the way.

Tom, Barbara, and I walked into our camp at around 5 P.M., glad the day had ended without any major problems.

My tent, literally frozen solid by now, was set by the side of the icy river. I put on every article of clothing I could find and slept sporadically. I woke up with a sore throat and had a tough time swallowing. With much reluctance I got out of my sleeping bag. The sun was up by the time we started on our unmarked trail, bushwhacking and crossing stretches of frozen creeks with ice-covered boulders.

After some confusion, we found a clear and comfortable path further up the mountain. Flowering trees and bushes covered the landscape below. The brook came alive under the bright sunshine, colliding giddily with glistening boulders and resuming its roaring, joyous song, accompanied along the way by a choir of vibrantly-colored birds.

At the foot of a narrow, suspended bridge, the Tibetan village of Ghunsa, dotted with cottages, appeared in distance.

In this isolated region of Nepal where villages are connected to the rest of the world only through narrow footpaths, bridges over torrential rivers are the most important means of transport. Most of the region's more modern bridges were built by the Swiss or the Canadians, and many of these structures were in need of repair. One bridge we crossed had lost part of its suspension support. It swayed side to side and up and down over the yawning chasm far below. No one seemed to know how much weight the bridge could hold. Its safety was tested by the Sherpas. First the lightest man went across. Then the next heaviest. Then the next and so on until it was determined that the feeble bridge could bear the weight, at least for now, of the heaviest of our group. The bridge creaked under me, and I felt as if I had just stepped over the edge of the world. Some fraying rope and splintering planks were all that stood between me and oblivion.

Late in the afternoon, we arrived in Ghunsa, a Tibetan village that is largely deserted during the winter.

We stayed in a two-story Sherpa inn with its recently painted doors of bright vibrant blue. The small inn was run by a family with five children. The family lived in a smoky room in the lower level that doubled as both kitchen and lounge where customers were severed tea and beer. Customers dropped in and out at anytime and sat around the fire where meals were prepared for the family. Beer was served in tall wooden containers filled with millet over which hot water was added periodically and drank through a straw.

David's knee was not getting any better. He decided to stay in Ghunsa and to be evacuated by helicopter.

I also opted to stay put in order to nurse my cold which by now was in full bloom with severe bronchitis chills and fever. Others decided to go beyond for two more days of exploration. There were three rooms upstairs; I rented the corner suite for fifty cents a night. A thin wall of plywood separated my suite from the next room. Wind blew through slats in the walls between the two rooms. The walls were adorned with pictures cut out of old magazines. There was a narrow cot in the corner. A noisy hen, cackling and bobbing her head, perched in a gap at the corner near the ceiling. I spent a couple of nights in Ghunsa Hilton.

With the help of aspirin, cough suppressants, and a hot water bottle, I slipped into my sleeping bag in the corner of the dark drafty room and soon fell asleep. I woke up a few times during the night. Once to the sound of porters laughing in the room next door. Once to the sound of cows and goats passing through the yard below. Another time to the barking of domesticated dogs and wild jackals.

A helicopter emerged from the clouds the following day and landed in a nearby field to evacuate David with now a badly swollen knee, unable to walk. There was pandemonium in the village. Everyone gathered around the chopper. I learned it was originally scheduled to evacuate Bob but could not because of the weather. It was easy to understand the difficulty that the rescue team encountered due to rapid and unpredictable changes of the weather in this region. I remembered how quickly the clouds had gathered when we were descending from the pass two days earlier and completely obscuring the earth beneath us, giving us an unearthly feeling of walking above the clouds.

Norbu informed us later the same day that Bob and Laurie were also evacuated and were taken to the Canadian clinic in Kathmandu.

We heard through Norbu, our only source of information to the outside world, who got his information from a static transistor radio in Tibetan language, that George W. Bush had won the 2000 U.S. election. Norbu told us about some problem with the vote-count, and we wondered what exactly was transpiring back in our home country.

From my diary in Ghunsa Hilton:

"The yak lamp is emitting a yellow-blue light and a lot of smoke as it twists and turns by the cold drafts crisscrossing the room from every corner. We were supposed to meet the lama at the monastery this morning, but I just heard that he could not join us since he had gone to find his yak. So we wait.

Norbu is a devout Buddhist. I have noticed him mumbling prayers when our group faces a risky situation. While waiting for the lama, Norbu gave us a synopsis about the Hindu mythology and its difference from Buddhism.

Good news. The lama has found his yak! Now we are off to the monastery on the other side of the river."

Sunshine filled the valley. The village began to stir as we crossed the roaring river on a flimsy wooden bridge. The path zigzagged through juniper bushes where goats and cows grazed. Outside the monastery the penetrating golden rays of sun were so inviting that I sat on a rock, silently absorbing the warmth of the sun and breathing in the mountain air. I meditated there for some time, watching the flocks of silver-winged pigeons darting across the azure sky. I wondered if they were the same ones that I used to observe from the coolness of my bed on the rooftop of my childhood home.

I thought of the young boy with a mythical name of Fraydoon, who was fascinated by their freedom and by their ability to soar, the young boy who imagined flying with them into the far reaches of the globe where he created his own world of dreams. Have those same birds come this far from my home in the alleys of southern Tehran to this remote village on the rooftop of the world?